I AM A WITNESS

Dreams and Visions of Dream

Volume.2

Willie Stanfield

authorHOUSE®

AuthorHouse™
1663 Liberty Drive
Bloomington, IN 47403
www.authorhouse.com
Phone: 1 (800) 839-8640

Published by AuthorHouse 03/30/2016

ISBN: 978-1-5246-0003-7 (sc)
ISBN: 978-1-5246-0002-0 (e)

Scripture quotations marked KJV are from the Holy Bible, King James Version (Authorized Version). First published in 1611. Quoted from the KJV Classic Reference Bible, Copyright © 1983 by Zondervan Corporation.

Print information available on the last page.

Any people depicted in stock imagery provided by Thinkstock are models, and such images are being used for illustrative purposes only. Certain stock imagery © Thinkstock.

This book is printed on acid-free paper.

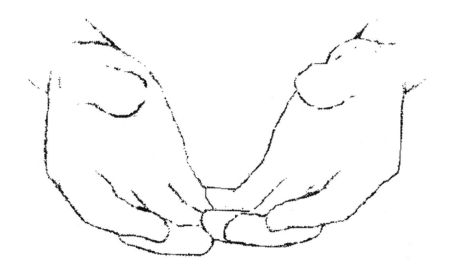

To My Beloved one, who enlightened
Me With
The Greatest Gift A Man Could Give To Another.
You Gave Me Your All, When You Demonstrated
The Gift Of
Knowing God, Through Your Walk In Life.

I Love You.

This book is an update on Dreams and Visions of Dreams.- Volume 1.

Volume.2, Gives proof, predictions, and documentation of Biblical Prophecy in history today, from Volume 1.

Volume.2 book, also reveal future dates from dreams of future events that will show proof in upcoming Volume 3.

Look for the next book Volume.3 in year 2020 as it will reveal volume.2, prophecy and the next End-Times World-Events, that will change the course of history in biblical prophecy.

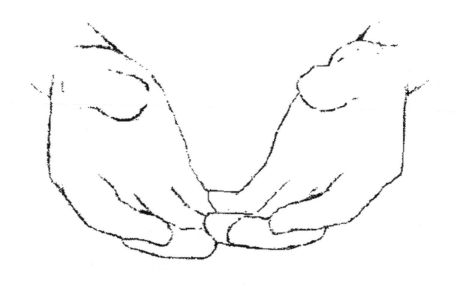

(KJV) Acts 2:16-17

16 But this is that which was spoken by the prophet Joel;

17 And it shall come to pass in the last days, saith God, I will pour out of my Spirit upon all flesh; and your sons and your daughters shall prophesy, and your young men shall see visions, and your old men shall dream dreams.

TABLE OF CONTENTS

Chapter 1 1

Chapter 2 33

Chapter 3 37

Chapter 4 107

Chapter 5 119

Chapter 6 129

Chapter 7 147

Chapter 8 165

Chapter 9 251

Chapter 10 263

CHAPTER 1

Dreams and Visions of Dreams

My journey on Earth is like the game of chess and the moves that are made guide me through each day in my walk. Chess is a game for two players who each move their sixteen pieces according to a set of rules across the board and try to trap and checkmate their opponent's kings.

I once knew a man who dreamt that he broke a vase. I told him, "Your dream was trying to warn you, so be careful or you'll break something eventually." The same day he was putting up dishes in his cabinet, and a dish fell to the floor and shattered into pieces. He had forgotten all about the dream and the warning.

I reminded him about the dream, but he denied any connection. He said the broken vase in the dream was an expensive one, and the dish he had broken had very little value.

Scripture teaches the virtues of having faith, knowledge, wisdom, and charity, the greatest being charity. However, the most important notion is that we must perceive the words of understanding.

The point is that the man would not accept the connection between the dream and the fact of what had occurred. He denied the dream because the value of the vase far exceeded the value of the dish he broke in reality. He did not understand that the value of the vase had no bearing on the dream. The value of what was broken in the dream was not important. Would a man be wiser if he walks through life with a blindfold? Only if he walks by faith and not by sight, is he wiser. Yes, a blind man who sees with understanding is wiser than a man with sight who is blind to reality.

My name is Will Stanfield. I'm just lying here trying to fall asleep. You may have had the feeling of your mind being so busy that you cannot go to sleep, and all you can do is just let your mind wander. But, I guess I should tell you a little about myself.

Let me take a moment to say my prayers before I fall asleep. I really need to stay connected with God. Oh, wait just a minute. The phone is ringing.

"Hello. Yes, this is he. No, I would not like to sign up for the daily newspaper. Why? I read the paper free on my job, and I read the paper at the library on the weekends. Hey, I'm sorry, but sometimes 'no' just means 'no.' Good-bye."

Oh my! pushy salespeople?

Now back to our conversation. This may sound a little strange to some people, but others may understand. I am a person who has dreams, and I see them at one point or another. I am a visionary. People may think my visions are impractical; however, my dreams are my God-given spiritual gift. Now don't misunderstand me—I'm not saying that I can predict the future, or that I'm a psychic. I'm just someone who is able to capture the essence of reality from my dreams.

I also feel the denial of my impulse of dreams and visions would be a denial of the spiritual realm that makes me human. Therefore, without vision, I'm limited only to sight with my eyes. Well, I'm getting a little sleepy now. The phone is ringing again. This salesperson is persistent.

"Hello," I said. But it wasn't the salesperson. "Good morning, Dr. Yu. My appointment is today at ten o'clock a.m.? I'll see you then. Thank you and good-bye."

Finally, my appointment is today. Maybe this psychologist can help me. These dreams are beginning to haunt me. I've been up all night. Couldn't sleep. Maybe I can rest an hour before my appointment. It is exactly eight o'clock.

I feel a bit nervous as I stand here knocking Dr. Yu's door. This is my first time meeting with a psychologist.

"Come in. Good morning, Mr. Stanfield," he says. Just have a seat. I am Dr. Yu. I will be with you in a minute. Go and take up a restful position on the couch and close your eyes."

I think this Dr. Yu is a very peculiar person. He did not get up from his seat or shake my hand.

He is sitting in his chair facing the window. His back is towards me. The only thing I can see is the color of his suit arm sleeve. He turns a little to pull a note pad from his desk. Well, you know, the old saying about first impressions being everything. This office is spooky. I have never seen so many stuffed animal heads in one room. This bearskin rug on the floor facing me is the most frightening of all, and he wants me to sit here and close my eyes. Maybe I should talk with him first, and then get a second opinion.

"Dr. Yu, why should I just close my eyes?"

"This would be for the purpose of self-observation and concentrated attention," says Dr. Yu. "I must view your thoughts as they come to the surface. Now, this is important. The success of my analysis depends upon you noting and communicating everything that passes through your mind. Now, you must not allow yourself to suppress even one thought, even if it seems to be unimportant or irrelevant to the subject."

He pauses—I suppose to let what he'd said sink in. He says in a kind voice.

"Mr. Stanfield, I would like to know a little about you. Go back as far as you can. What do you remember?"

I'll tell you the story just as I told Dr. Yu.

There's not much that I can remember. The first thing I can remember is between the ages of five and six. I was sitting down at a little school desk and I began to draw on a sheet of paper. I can remember it as if it were yesterday. It was my hand that stroked the pencil, but it was as if a greater power was guiding me. As I began to draw, I realized what a remarkable picture it was. I realized this to be a talent that was given from God. I realized from that point that I could draw anything I saw, and I could draw at least half of anything I could envision.

"Well! Mr. Stanfield," Dr. Yu says. If any, tell me about the first failure you can remember, and what affect it had on your life."

I remember my second-grade teacher who I only remember by name and not by face. The reason I probably remember her by name is because of the impression she left upon me. Every time she disciplined me, she would strike me in the palm of my hand with a ruler and then ask me.

"What is my name?"

"Mrs. Abby," I said.

"Miss Abby. That's right Miss Abby, the teacher. That's Miss—M.I.S.S. Abby. Now, hold out your hand."

She would spell her name out as she hit me in the hand: M—whack, I—whack, S—whack . . . right on through A-B-B-Y. This was quite often and at times, she would warn me not to pull my hand back. Then she would make me spell my name as she hit me in the hand with the ruler: W-I-L-L-I-E S-T-A-N-F-I-E-L-D—twenty-three whacks altogether. She would then ask me, "Who are you? What's your name?'"

"Willie Stanfield"

"Spell it."

"W-I-L-L-I-E S-T-A-N-F-I-E-L-D."

"Don't you forget. Now sit down."

The palms of my hands would burn and burn and burn. But I didn't cry.

The last time I remember her disciplining me when I disobeyed her in the classroom was for talking. She made me stay in the room for recess—a normal procedure for punishment. When everyone was out for recess with the teacher, she'd lock the door and leave the window open.

Well, as you can imagine, opportunity was knocking at the window for me as I saw my friends playing on the outside. I jumped out of the window to play with them. I must have forgotten about my punishment. As the students went into the room, I went in with them and she was standing just inside the door, waiting patiently.

She had the ruler in one hand, patting it in the other.

"Hold out your hand."

My palms had cooled somewhat, but they were fat from swelling.

I held out my hand. For every word she asked me, she hit me in the hand.

"Who—whack—am—whack—I? Whack"

"Miss Abby the teacher."

"And—whack—who—whack—are—whack—you? Whack."

"Willie Stanfield."

"What are you?"

"The student," I replied. I wondered how many questions she could dream up.

"What did I tell you to do?"

"Stay in the room."

I stood there and tap-danced as she hit me in the center of my hand with the ruler. By the time I finished second grade, I was able to spell my name backwards. My hands got tough, too.

Well, I did repeat second grade because my parents thought I would learn my greatest lesson by this and take school seriously. My teacher thought I was just going through a phase that would pass. In fact, it did change my whole outlook on life and school, and I never failed in school again.

I paused to see the psychologist's reaction.

"All right, Mr. Stanfield," he says.

"Tell me about the first dream you can remember. Go back as far as you can."

When the first dream occurred, I don't remember my age. I didn't understand it at the time. This may seem somewhat strange. This is the only dream I remember. In this dream, I was standing in front of an audience. I was showing a poster of a drawing. I won a first-place ribbon.

As I became a teenager, I saw myself in this dream painting and drawing with tools in my hand, making animals with clay and pouring liquids into little plaster forms. In the last part of this dream, all I remember is walking down the ramp and being on a stage receiving certificates of honor, and on another occasion, receiving awards of recognition for my talents. Looking back, I now understand this dream to be a vision of future events.

When I examine this dream, I look back in elementary school. I was in the 4-H club and had weekly poster contests. The students would compete from all classes in second grade to sixth grade, and I would win these contests with first-place ribbons quite often. I also remember a disappointing moment when I came in second place.

At this time, I was out of school on the sick list and could not be there for competition. My poster was entered into the contest, anyway. On contest days, students would stand in front of the club leaders and family members who were there to see the display of posters. I lay sick in my bed on this particular day and remember my classmate came by to visit me after school, and I can remember as if it were yesterday the first words that came out of her mouth.

"Are you ok?"

"Did I win?"

She looked at me and smiled.

"You won second place."

I don't know why I was so disappointed in myself. Maybe I felt it was one of my best drawings of the 4-H events and I thought maybe if I'd been there, I could've won first place. But now that I think about it. It would not have been ethical to give a first-place award to a student who was not there, even if it was the best drawing. Also, when you have sixty or more parents present and receiving award, politics takes precedence over ethics.

As I became older and went off to junior high in grades seventh through ninth, I received certificates, one after another, in all classes and in different forms of arts and crafts. By the time I was in high school, I continued to make excellent grades in my arts and crafts classes. I also helped friends that did not have the gift of drawing. It all came very easy to me, and I did not understand why so many students struggled with these classes.

I was able to make friends by helping. I also made quite an impression on the young ladies helping them out with drawing. Hey! If I'm going to use my talent, I may as well use it to my advantage. So, at the end of the dream, I recognized now that this was my senior year of high school, and I was in every art and architectural drafting class. In every class, I performed exceptionally well.

By this time, my abilities and talents for the arts were beyond measure. I knew I had a talent for the arts. I also remember that in my painting class, my instructor gave me the duty of collecting the paintings at the end of the day. Often, I collected the paintings to put in the storeroom, and students would ask me to help them fix their paintings. You would have thought some of these were abstract paintings, but this was not their intention. I amazed myself because at the stroke of the brush, I was able to bring life to the paintings that had no chance for a decent grade.

As I stood there with very little time at the end of class, I was stocking paintings and fixing them at the same time. I was not the smartest out of the group, but I was probably the most talented. Much to my surprise, at the end of the year on high school honors night, I was asked to participate in the ceremony.

On the stage of honors night, I was recognized with the best of the best at all academic levels. As I estimate, of a student body of approximately 2,200 students, only about 25 to 30 students sat on that stage for honors night. This was a great honor, but no surprise to me as to why I was there. When the category began for all class instructors to present awards, I was called up to the platform and recognized for the category of arts.

To my surprise, my name was called again and again in the arts category. The only honor I didn't receive was in the category of architectural drafting, but I was second runner-up. In addition to these awards, I attended two schools at the same time. On weekends and during the summer, I was in a special program on the college campus of Southern University of Baton Rouge, Louisiana.

From seventh grade to 12th grade, I attended two schools on a regular basis. For five years, I had the best experience of my life growing up. I had the opportunity to meet students from all areas of the parish, and stayed on the Southern University campus in the summer with other university students.

My adorable aunt, Ms. Thomas, was a program teacher who introduced me to the program. She was also my first English instructor in my first semester of college. I will always remember the day my aunt sat on the bed studying her books in an endeavor to complete her higher degree of education. I kneeled down by the bed as she studied when I was only a boy of 12 or 13.

The words she spoke to me one particular day would define me. They gave me the opportunity to mold my personality and become part of the man I am today.

She said, "I have something in mind for you that I think you should try."

"What?"

"I think you can use some inspiration that will help mold you and give you some other activities to do. I think you will like it."

She introduced me to the Upward Bound Program on the campus of Southern University. During my first summer in the program, I was the youngest student because my aunt was able to talk to the director and get me in early. I thought of myself as a laid back guy and I liked to observe everything. Some people may have seen me as shy and reserved. My dreams and visions at this time were infrequent and not memorable. The series of events didn't seem to pile up until they got to a warning point. After this, they commenced to have some import, as you will see before long.

The second summer in Upward Bound, I talked Craig into enrolling as well. Craig attended McKinley High. We were always very close. We would spend practically the whole summer together. I would stay with him on the south side of town, either before or after I came back from Pensacola. Craig and I had good times in the program, meeting many good people.

A couple of our good friends were Jack and Dean, who also attended McKinley High. Jack was a very interesting person who was a great tennis player for the school. He had a 4.0 grade point average and planned on going to medical school. Jack and I had to get accustomed to each other because we were just beginning to know one another. Jack and, sometimes, Dean often would run to catch up with Craig and me on our way to breakfast. Jack was a great student, but often slept late until we began to wake him up. Craig would get a big kick out of Jack and me picking at each other. Jack would often initiate it, but most of the time, I would catch him off guard.

"Come on Jack," I would say. "Do you ever comb your hair in the morning? You can't hang with us like that. A man with your intelligence can't get out the bed in the morning with your head looking like this and think it's natural. I know it's called 'a natural,' but you just don't naturally refuse to comb it."

"Look you red-head, cornbread eating . . . Look here! Don't start with me this morning. I haven't had my breakfast yet, and you are starting with me already. I can't handle you on an empty stomach."

Craig would start our day like that, laughing at Jack and me. Dean was an interesting character in his own right. He was somewhat of a settled guy, but had a very deep speech impediment. We all thought it was funny at first. I felt sorry after a while, but Craig could never control himself. It got to the point where I would beg Craig not to laugh at Dean before we met up with him in the morning. Craig would promise me every morning he wouldn't laugh and I think some mornings he would earnestly try. Nevertheless, each morning, Dean would run up to us and begin to speak, and I would think if he could just get the first word out without stuttering, maybe Craig could control himself. That never happened. Once Dean began to try to talk, I would briefly glimpse at Craig and shake my head a little to tell Craig,

"No."

That is all it took for Craig to get started. What got me more than anything was that I knew once he started laughing, I would laugh.

"Man," I would say, "stop, please. I asked you not to do that. You see you've got me laughing too."

Well, I didn't feel too bad because Dean would start laughing with us.

My last three years in the program were amazing, and I was beginning to develop higher interpersonal education. By the time I was a junior and senior, I was not as shy as before. I began to be more assertive and aggressive in my activities. It did not matter whether I was in the classroom answering questions or asking questions. I made higher marks on grades. I was more aggressive with sports activities, and approaching the young ladies and walking them to the dormitory after school.

In my last summer in the program, I roomed with Marvin, and we became the best of friends. He attended Capital High School, and I attended Istrouma High School in the regular season. I often went to his house on the weekends when we were off campus. We played basketball every chance we got. He was very active on the sports teams in school and he often tried to get me to play because I was just as competitive as he in sports. However, I had no interest in organized sports activities at this time.

Some of the other guys that hung out with us as a group were John and Darnell from Scotlandville High. Antwawn, Timothy, and Frank were from Istrouma high. Last, but not least, was the big, tall guy from Waterloo, Iowa. We just called him "Waterloo." There was rumor that his family was a prominent family from upstate and that they came down South to visit other upstanding friends of the family. In the middle of the school season, he was able to get into the program with no problem when other students could not. It was also rumored that his family was the reason the program was able to afford the elaborate, unexpected trip to Texas. We went to see the Houston Astor's play and attended Six Flags over Texas due to a healthy donation from his family. I remember saying to Marvin that we should form a pact with the group, and I think it was Marvin who came up with name "The Hounds" because we were always on the go. We came up with the idea to wear t-shirts with the group name on them. Within three weeks, we began to see others from the program that had group names on the back of their t-shirts. Another group was "Solid Gold." We also began eventually to see college students with their group names as well.

This group of guys hung out together in the girls' lobby and played ping-pong and other games as we listened to music. After class and lunch, there were time requirements for activities we had to attend. Our day was planned to keep us occupied as a unit. We were responsible for study hall, organized sports, games, and inside recreation. It was a requirement for everyone to participate in these activities. One month we would play baseball, the next bowling, and then volleyball.

This is where I met a very interesting female companion. During our sports activities, my group would play volleyball next to the football stadium. I would walk away from the group into the stadium at times and sit as I would wait for the next game to play. I knew the college's track team was practicing here. This is where I met the interesting track star from Ft. Lauderdale, Florida. I went to the track field and observed her running for maybe three days before we began to talk. She was very interesting to me because of her phenomenal speed. Her speed showed me that she did not run the long distance. The quick relay and 100-yard dash were her specialties. She was a very pretty lady of dark complexion with very defined legs that showed she was a runner.

I began to notice her around campus and at morning breakfast. She was always by herself when I saw her. One day, I saw her walk into the cafeteria as I was sitting with friends at breakfast.

"John, there she is," I said. "I met her on the track field.'"

"Oh, that's her?"

"Yes, that's her. I'm going over to sit with her."

"I don't believe you."

She was very well dressed this day and she looked extremely enticing. My friends were surprised to see me stand up with my food tray and move from the table away from them. I went to sit with her and the look on some of the students' faces was a Kodak moment. Even more of an astonishing look was on the faces of the young females because they did not think I knew her. What amazed me was to learn that some women are not interested or attracted to you until they see you with someone else. I think it's the mystery of wanting to know what other people find interesting in you. The next day at the table, one of the young females asked me a question in an interesting fashion.

"Is that your friend?" she asked.

"Maybe. Why do you ask?"

"She's pretty."

"Thank you."

My newfound friend and I were becoming very close and began to spend a lot of time together. I thought this was very pleasant because I was able to spend time alone with her away from my peers. I was able to attend some of the college dances and events with her when my peers could not. Our relationship was very mature and so easy-going that it seemed as if we were made for one another.

Then one day, a turn of events came about when we returned to her dorm from a walk around campus. Her room was on the first floor. I walked her to the door and we stood by the rail close to the door. She then invited me into her room and we sat and talked for some time. We played around on her bed a little, and then went back onto the sidewalk next to her room. The head of women's residence was in the front area close to my friend's room. The house residence lady approached us in front of the room with an attitude that caught us off guard.

My friend and I were not aware of the policies of having guests in the rooms. She was under the impression that because she was in the senior dormitory, she was permitted to have a guest in her room. This was correct, because, guests were required to check in first. By the time the head of ladies finished with us, my friend had a three-month curfew and I had to mop the girls' lobby and her office for three months. She also tried to antagonize my friend and tried often to make her uncomfortable. She began to speak to me, especially when she saw us together. My friend was not going to put up with this for too long. She said that if she could not get a transfer to another dorm, she was not going to return after the Christmas break. I missed her because we had good times together and really had good chemistry. She went back to South Florida, and like most relationships when young lovers are distant, ours faded away into the night like a sunset.

The next summer was the last of the summer programs for me. I did not have a relationship that developed as this one did, but I had fun trying. I did stay within the boundaries of the program, as I found several young girls in my peer group interesting. Most of the students, by this time, had been in the program for a few years, and we knew of each other well. Some of the girls were like best friends. Nevertheless, I could not help but become closer than friends with some.

One young girl who attended Scotlandville High was a basketball player for the school, and we both admired each other on the ball court. She had very pretty brown eyes and a pretty little brown frame to match. We had very little time to spend with each other because we were headed towards the end of the school year when an incident occurred that encouraged many parents to pull away from the program. One of our peers was shot on campus. This frightens most parents. The last thing I remember was saying goodbye to her and telling her how much I would miss her as we just held each other.

After that relationship, many of my friends and I began our first semester of college. We were in the last quarter of the Upward Bound program. One of my last relationships toward the end of the semester was with a young lady that I was just beginning to know. We did not have much of a chance to grow as a couple. We were almost there as we began to hang out and when students saw us, they always saw us together. She was very attractive and was a cheerleader for her school. I saw that some of the girls resented her. We were getting very close but we were not quite a couple yet because she actually had a friend off campus who attended her high school. I think she was in the process of breaking up with him. She was giving me the signs more and more often, but she never gave me notions of a final break-off. It seemed as though she wanted both worlds. Maybe she wanted the football star, but she was letting me know that she was really falling for me. I could feel the turn of the relationship as she was beginning to become possessive in front of other females. Then a turn of events occurred. She wanted to tell me something just before this particular incident, but we never had a chance to talk.

On one night, the campus had a blackout and the lights were out over the entire campus. It was late and my roommate Marvin received a phone call from one of the girls who was interested in him. She asked him to come to her room, as it was the perfect opportunity since no one could see him when it was pitch dark. There were other girls in the room next to her, and one of the girls asked the guy from Waterloo, Iowa to come and see her. There was one other girl in the room and she asked me to come to the room and visit her.

I began to think Marvin was very advanced in the routine of sneaking in the girls' dorm. As I thought about it, I realized there were some nights when Marvin was not in his bed until late in the night. Another guy by the name of Darnel got wind of what was happening and wanted to go along even though he didn't have a girl lined up. Maybe he thought he would find a date once we got there. Security was swarming like bees on this night because of the blackout, but Marvin knew of an underground route to avoid them.

We ran from our building to another one that was vacant, then jumped up and grabbed the rail to the first floor. We wanted to stay clear of the open field. We ran through the halls and stopped occasionally to let security pass by. From that building to the next building we ran to the girls' dorm, jumped up and grabbed the rails to pull ourselves up. There we had to hide one more time to avoid security and let them pass. Then we ran up to the second floor to the girls' room.

When we were all in the girls' rooms, Marvin went with his friend to the next room. Waterloo and I remained in the first room on the girls' bed and Darnel just sat in the chair. We all were doing our own little thing, as it was completely dark in the room. We were all in the room about twenty minutes when we heard a knock at the door. I became a bit frantic for I thought it was security or the ladies' dorm keeper checking on the girls.

"Are you going to answer that?"

My friend went to the door.

"Who is it?" she said.

She came back to the bed.

"It's for you," she told me.

"For me? It can't be."

I went to the door. It was my friend who I hung out with a lot.

She said, "I want you to come to my room."

Then she walked away and I went back to the bed.

"I guess I don't have to ask how she knew I was here," I said.

"I told her you were coming to see me."

"But why, when you were the one that asked me to come over?"

"Because I can't stand her and I know she likes you."

"So you used me to get to her."

She became silent and did not say anything.

"Well, I guess I will go to her room," I said. Do you want me to go?"

"No."

I looked at her and took a deep breath. Then there was another knock on the door. I went to the door.

"Well, are you coming?" my friend asked?

"No, I'm going to stay here with the group. All of the guys are in here."

I wanted to go, but I also wanted to stay. I was between a rock and a hard place. What forced my decision was that she did not have her mind made up in the first place to be with me. Also, going back to her room was only the result of my being in Mavis' room and that motive did not suit me well. I don't know what conversation they had on the phone, but it seems as though I was the only one out of the loop.

The next month, before the program ended for the summer, I experienced my first premonition. This was a warning of anticipating an event without a conscious notion. I began to realize there was something truly strange about my dreams, which I had tried to ignore for a long time. I just did not understand. Up to this moment, I had seen people hold onto their hopes and dreams all their lives without them ever becoming reality. I began to see my dreams appear and hoped I would not see my destruction in my sleep.

One night I was sleeping when I began to hear things without any images of what was happening—only voices and screams, then the sound of a gunshot and one last scream. This was the end of this dream, and then I awakened from this dream. I sat up and as I looked around I realized I was in my bed and my roommate was in his bed asleep. I was wet with sweat, my heart pounding in my chest, my head, and my ears.

Two days later I saw my dream become a reality. The day started normally enough. I woke up that morning and went to breakfast with the crew. We attended school and afterwards went to lunch. After lunch, we went to the dorm to get some rest. Four hours later sports and recreational activities began.

After recreation, we were on our way back to the dorm when two guys and I stopped in front of the girls' dorm. We saw one of our schoolmates known as "Football." He was from the home school of McKinley High and was a high profile football player. We walked up to Football as he was talking to one of the three guys from off campus from the Scotlandville area. Then I heard Football say, "So you are the one I heard that came to the dorm and aggravated my friend."

"So what?"

"So you need to stop hanging around here."

"Who's going to make me?"

Then Football, with a golf ball in his hand, punched the teenager from off campus in the mouth and knocked him out. After a minute or so his friends helped him up off the ground and they left the area.

A few hours later, it began to get dark and a mandatory meeting was called for 7:30 p.m. I was beginning to have some very strange feelings about this incident as we were on our way back to the girls' dorm for the meeting. I said,

"Look man, I don't feel good about what happened today with Football. We need to go back to the dorm and prepare for this."

"No man, don't even worry about that. They aren't coming back."

"Ok, man."

I said no more about the incident as we were on our way to the meeting. It was now approximately 7:30, and we were all gathered in the small lobby of the girl's dorm. About two hundred students were in the lobby area. As the dorm leader began to speak, three guys walked in. One of the boys went to the middle of the floor and pointed at the dorm leader.

"You're the one who brought these outsiders in here from downtown," he said.

Marvin and I stood up. The dorm leader told us to sit down but the intruder stood in the middle of the floor. He turned around to look across the room and then he pulled out a gun. The crowd of students panicked and ran. One of the girls ran into me and frantically pushed me to a corner. I took her out the door and we ran. When it was all over, Football was shot in the head five times with a .22-caliber air gun. Fortunately, he survived and was able to have all but one of the bullets pulled out.

The next day my roommate and I did not go to class, as we were concerned about Football's outcome. We were trying to make calls and get some information when there was a knock on the door. It was the program assistance director who came by to check on us and let everyone know that Football was doing well. After we knew he was okay, we were fine and it was as if a weight was lifted off my shoulders.

Only one week and one last dance remained before the end of the summer. We dedicated this dance to Football and could feel the vibe from the group as we chanted his name at the closing of the party. On our way back to the dorms, a small group of us walked our usual route. We were about fifty feet from the over-path we had to cross to get to the dorms. I said to Marvin, "It looks like we've got company.

"It's another crew from off campus," Marvin said.

"Grab the girls. Don't let them walk across by themselves."

Marvin, John, a few others, and I took the hands of the girls as we walked towards the bridge. I took the lead. I talked with the female as we walked to calm her down. She was very frightened as we walked towards the bridge.

"Oh no, not again," she said.

"Don't be afraid. Just keep walking."

"But I'm scared."

"It'll be okay. I've got you."

She gripped my hand very tightly. Her hand shook with fear as we walked across the bridge. Before we knew it there were guys on both side of the six-foot wide bridge, and we had to walk about one hundred feet to the other side. They just looked at us and we looked at them and kept walking. Then one of the other guys said,

"My tennis shoes are brand new and I just got out of jail. Just don't step on my shoes. I don't mind going back."

We just kept walking. We walked the girls right past both sets of guys all the way to the dorm.

"Thank you so much, she said. I was so scared."

"You see. I told you everything would be ok. Can I see you tomorrow?"

"I want to very much, but I can't stay because of the shooting."

"It sounds like we may not get to see each other again."

"I know, she said and I want to see you, but it's curfew time. I have to go."

So I embraced her. The only thing that broke us apart was a student that came around the corner and startled us. Princess seemed to be just as surprised as we were. We then stared into each other's eyes as we said goodbye and continued to hold hands as she walked away slowly until we released at arms' length. Then I stood and watched her walk away and I never saw her again.

Only two days remained before the school term was over. I knew I was going to miss the best times and people I have ever experienced in my life. I received a surprise visit from a young lady who came to the boys' dorm. There were hollering sounds in the hallway that came from some of the guys. I ignored it because some of the guys were always running around in the halls up to no good. I heard a knock on the door. It was Darnel to inform me that I had a female visitor who wanted to see me at the end of the hall. This was a surprise because we were on the fourth floor and girls did not come up the stairs or elevator as far as I knew.

I came to find that she came in the boy's dorm by herself and waited for me at the end of the hall where she had walked up four flights of stairs. I walked to the end of the hall to meet her and walked back to my room with her to get my jacket so I could walk her back downstairs. There were too many guys who knew she was upstairs so I wanted to get downstairs before she got in trouble. She was a very attractive female and I had no idea she was interested in me until that day. The guys could not believe she came to see me. I was just as surprised as they were. As we walked back down the stairs, we talked.

"This is quite a surprise," I said. What made you come up here?"

"I've wanted to tell you for a long time that I had a crush on you."

"Why did you wait so long?"

"I don't know. I guess I was a little shy, and I didn't know how to tell you."

"It took a lot of nerve to come in the boys' dorm and tell me this way."

"Well, we only have two days left in the program and I thought I would never get a chance to say what was on my mind. I decided, once I made up my mind, that I would let you know in an impressive way."

"Well I'm impressed," I said.

I was attracted to her, but we didn't have a chance to spend time together because it was the last night of the program before moving back home. The only time we were able to spend time together was the day of returning home. I went to her room to help her bring luggage down. We spent time in the room as we waited on her ride to pick her up, for this was the only day that the males were allowed to go in the rooms to help. Everyone was asked to keep the doors open while in the rooms. Well, we had a long talk and I gave her a back rub, or, I would say, a full therapeutic massage. We talked until her ride came and I took her bags down to the car. After all, I am a gentleman.

At the end of the year an instructor by the name of Mr. Tucker was fascinated by my artwork. He was a professor of World History and Literature. He was an extraordinary man. I was inspired by his method of teaching and motivation. I was also fascinated with him as a professor and I thought he was the coolest guy I had ever met.

This man had everything going for himself and was very intelligent. I wanted someday to be just like him. Mr. Tucker admired my artwork tremendously. He set up a display room to show my work to other art and literature classes as part of a class project. On honors night I received five awards. Only one plaque was awarded that I didn't receive. That award went to a very good friend of mine—Princess. She deserved that award and maybe one or two more.

"Princess later became a very close friend when we went off to the same junior college, but that's another story," I said to the psychiatrist.

I looked at him. The desk phone rang. It was quite strange. Dr. Yu didn't turn around to answer the phone. He reached back and pulled the phone to him and his pen fell to the floor. I still couldn't see his face as he rolled back his chair with his feet and picked up his pen. He said,

"You are a man with a special talent, and you have a spiritual gift."

He began to write on his note pad the word "talent" in large letters.

God continues to work with man in many
ways as he did in biblical days.

Mt. 25:14

For the kingdom of heaven is as a man traveling into a far
country, who called his own servants, and delivered unto
them his goods.

Mt. 25:15

And unto one he gave five talents, to another two, and to
another one; to every man according to his several ability;
and straightway took his journey.

Mt. 25:16

Then he that had received the five talents went and traded
with the same, and made them other five talents.

Mt. 25:19

After a long time the lord of those servants cometh, and
reckoned with them.

Mt. 25:20

And so he that had received five talents came and brought
other five talents, saying, Lord, thou deliveredst unto me
five talents: behold, I have gained beside them five talents
more.

Mt. 25: 21

His lord said unto him, Well done, thou good and faithful servant: thou hast been faithful over a few things, I will make thee ruler over many things: enter thou into the joy of thy lord.

CHAPTER 2

With Dr. Yu's back still turned to me, I continued.

In this dream, I saw myself poverty-stricken with very little money in my wallet. As the dream went on, I continued to look through my wallet, and my money began to deteriorate. Everything in the dream was spinning very fast and the dream was showing me a lot of signs but no details. I saw myself walking along the street with nothing to do and very few opportunities. Work was very light in a town of retirees and light industrial work. Employment was mostly industrial work and seasonal. I was going from job to job. I saw myself in slow motion in my room packing my bags and cleaning.

I was talking to a friend, shaking hands and saying good-bye. I also saw myself in the dream in a dispute with a female friend, saying I had to go. I saw myself sitting down and feeling a sad loss, unhappy. I began to see myself traveling a long journey, not knowing how far I had to go. This trip felt as if it was a never-ending journey, and I saw a road that had no end. On this journey, I found no comfort, and I began to see myself sleep within a dream.

As I began to see myself asleep in this dream, I saw water fountains flowing with high-rise water shooting in the sky. The fountains continued to flow streams of water, and it seemed as though they would never stop. I felt a sense of peace, and happiness. I felt as if I had finally met my destiny and then I awakened from this dream.

Dr. Yu at this time continued to sit in his chair. His back was towards me. He said,

"Sometimes in life, we have to leave the things we love the most to find a balance in our own life."

I finished telling the dream to Dr. Yu. I opened my eyes quietly as I heard a different voice. It was the bearskin rug. It said, "But this was spoken by the prophet Joel.

'And it should come to pass in the last days,' says God, 'I will pour out my spirit on all flesh; your sons and your daughters shall prophesy, your young men shall see visions, and your old men shall dream dreams.'"

The last thing I heard was Acts 2:16. I looked around at Dr. Yu. I said nothing about the rug. I didn't want Dr. Yu to think I was out of my mind. I looked at Dr. Yu again. He continued to sit in his chair with his back towards me. He began to write on his note pad the word "necessity" in large letters.

God continues to work with man in many
ways as he did in biblical days.

Genesis 19:19

Behold now, thy servant hath found grace in thy sight, and
thou hast magnified thy mercy, which thou hast showed
unto me in saving my life; and I cannot escape to the
mountain, lest some evil take me, and I die:

Genesis 19:20

Behold now, this city is near to flee unto, and it is a little
one: Oh, let me escape thither, (is it not a little one?) and
my soul shall live.

CHAPTER 3

"Mr. Stanfield, you seem to be a man with Christian values," Dr. Yu said.

"What is your outlook on the connection between God and man, and why do you compare your life to that of a chess game?"

I think all things in life are made up of negative and positive components. Just as a car battery has a negative, and a positive post. Without the negative post the battery has no energy. I feel this is like the connection with man and religion. If I did not have God, my soul would have no energy.

My journey on earth is like the game of chess, and the moves that are made seem to guide me through my daily walk in life. I have not made it this far on my own.

The game of chess is played between opponents who move pieces alternately on a square board. The objective is to place the opponent's king under subjection in such a way that the opponent has no legal move which would avoid the capture of his king on the following move. The player who achieves this is said to have checkmated the opponent and have won the game. The opponent who has been checkmated has lost the game.

God has made every man on earth a free agent. I have freedom of choice. I have the choice to serve one and despise the other, but I cannot serve two masters. I feel sometimes there are moves that are made for me on my behalf. The two opponents who move pieces alternately on my chessboard of life are God and Satan.

God is of truth and righteousness, and Satan is the opposite. I feel the greatest weapon of God with man is his church. For there is power in numbers, and "where there are two or more are gathered together in God's name, there he is in the midst." The pieces of the chess game are as follows:

1 King
1 Queen
2 Bishops
2 Rooks
2 Knights
8 Pawns

As I look at my journey in life I envision the body of Christ as the church. I envision the king as representing man's soul. The objective of the game is to place the opponent's king or soul under subjection and the opponent must avoid the capture of the king or man's soul on the following move, which is checkmate.

The queen moves to any square on the board in any direction like the elder who watches over the congregation and makes decisions for the congregation. With wisdom and experience, the queen, like the elder, attempts to lead the people in the right direction.

Bishops move to any square along a diagonal on which it stands like a pastor who ministers to the church and preaches from the pulpit of the church.

The knights move to one of the squares nearest to that on which it stands but not on the same rank, file, or diagonal. It does not pass directly over any intervening square. The knight is as a teacher, who teaches with his biblical knowledge. Sunday school teachers guide different levels of classes. This may consist of beginners or advanced classes under the rank of the ministry.

Pawns each move forward to the unoccupied square immediately in front of it and on the same file like a new member or a new-convert member learning for the first time. A pawn is one of the chessmen having the power to move only forward, ordinarily one square at a time, to capture only diagonally forward. It may be promoted to any piece except a king upon reaching the eighth rank. It is one that can be use to further the purpose of another.

When a pawn reaches the rank farthest from its starting position, it can advance as a queen, rook, bishop or knight. This exchange of a pawn for another piece is called a promotion and the effect of the new piece is immediate.

A pawn, in this case, is like a new member of the church who continues to grow and study to show himself approved so that he can be promoted and move up in the ranks. Therefore, when all members come together in the church, everyone is on one accord. In Greek terminology, this means "souls and souls together," which creates a spiritual fellowship.

Therefore, the Church is one of God's greatest weapons of defense.

Last but not least, is the opposition, Satan? The largest weapon of Satan is the undertaking of illusions. He is the master of illusions, and uses those illusions to intellectually deceive or mislead you. An illusion is the perception of something objectively existing in such a way as to cause misinterpretation of its actual nature. Satan is the great illusionist and he has his church of demons. This master demon, in his biggest offense, has made man think that what he is doing is right. The fact is that, in most cases, man is doing it the wrong way. Satan will cause man to look at meaningless things in the realms of salvation and create an illusion in order to delude him from grasping the simple facts that lead to salvation.

History is for our learning, and one of the greatest lessons I see in biblical teaching of worship service is this example:

> Leviticus 9:6-8; 10:1-2
> And Moses said, "This is the thing which the LORD commanded that ye should do; and the glory of the LORD shall appear unto you." / And Moses said unto Aaron, "Go unto the altar, and offer thy sin offering, and thy burnt offering, and make atonement for thyself, and for the people. And make atonement for them, as the Lord commanded."
>
> And Nadab and Abihu, the sons of Aaron, took either of them his censer, and put fire therein, and put incense thereon and offered strange fire before the Lord, which he commanded them not. / And there went out fire from the Lord and devoured them, and they were destroyed before the Lord.

In this history lesson I realized the Lord gave specific instructions on how he required the people to give their offerings of service. Every command was carried out completely, except one. The two men did not get the fire offering from the place where the Lord had commanded. In society, it is quite common for man to think fire is fire, as long as it gets the job done. I think, even under good intentions, if I were to add or take a little away from God's word, it is not acceptable. If God instructs me when to worship, how to give, when I must take communion, or the way I must sing, then I must do this accordingly without waiver.

In some cases, man has become very relaxed in his own self-judgment. For example, man will say, 'I don't have to do this or that to be of God,' or 'God knows my heart,' or 'No one know me but God.' I say, yes, God knows man's heart, and no one but God will have the final say in the end. Be not deceived; God is not mocked. Whatsoever his Word says, so shall it be.

In the book of Hosea the fourth chapter, it is stated:

Hear the word of the Lord, ye Israel; for the Lord hath a controversy with the inhabitants of the land, because there is no truth, nor mercy, nor knowledge of God in the land.

Hosea 4:6 states:

My people are destroyed for lack of knowledge; I will also reject thee, that thou hast forgotten the law of thy God I will also forget thy off spring.

In the end, I say every knee shall bow, and God shall have the final say over all men by the deeds done in the body according to His law. We should always pray for wisdom and understanding, lest Satan should gain an advantage on us, for God's will is not to have us ignorant of Satan's devices.

Paul stated in the church,

"I had rather speak five words with understanding, that by my voice I may teach others also, than ten thousand words in a tongue not known."

I have heard that a picture speaks a thousand words, but I say that with one word of understanding, I can show you a thousand pictures. God's wisdom is not of this world, and God's Word teaches me that if you lack wisdom, you are to ask it of Him. God tells us that His ways are not our ways, and His thoughts are not our thoughts. For I say, with man's thoughts, he can only go back in his mind, but with God's thoughts, he can go back in time.

I once heard that time is of the essence. God's Word says that one day to us can be as a thousand years unto the Lord. For I say, man can only control time on his wrist, but God has time in the palm of his hand. Man's ways are variable, but God's ways are constant and everlasting.

In conclusion, I think the key to Satan's illusion is to create a false impression. He wants man to think what he is doing is right. Therefore, man will feel no need to fix something that is not broken. If this continues, God can give man up to a reprobate mind and man will not believe.

I think this illusion from the Prince of Darkness will take a third of the earth with him.

We find in the story of the book of Denial, God supported and blessed the Jews of the Hebrew Israelite out of Judea. God answered every pray and protected Daniel, Mechick,

Seddrick, and Abednego against Nebicknezer gods of Zeus even in captivity.

I want to share with you a foretelling of events which began in 597 BC and proved triumphant. The future End-Times events in the book of Denial, where it is foretold that the great nations of the world will rise against the Lord; as God protected His people and His Kingdom. In The Book of Daniel he exhibited his faith and trust as God answered every prayer Denial asked of him. The story of Daniel includes his heroism, faith, and character in remaining faithful to God in the midst of an adverse and idolatrous culture. God remained loyal answering every prayer in protection of his faithful ones through his Angels and the young Jewish prophet who refused to participate in the idolatrous practices and customs of ancient World, following the captivity and exile.

This is an example of why man today must obey and practice the TRUTH totally, according to the purity in the word of God. The prophet Ezekiel, who wrote his prophecy about the same time mentioned three Biblical figures in a row as men of righteousness: Noah, Daniel, and Job (Ezekiel 14:14 and 14:20). The Son of man, Christ, referred to Daniel as the Prophet (Matthew 24:15).

The story of the Book in Chapters 1-6 refers to the trials of Daniel and his three young companions: Hananiah, Mishael, and Azariah, during the time of the great Kings of the East. Their names, all of which reflect the name of God, are changed by the rulers of the time and given names referring to idols and we must be cautious of modern-day-world concerning the change of holy names and scriptures today.

According to "Smithsonian Magazine by Kenneth C. Davis" October 2010, as the source where in my full research in America History.

(America's History of Religious Tolerance) The idea that the United States has always been a bastion of religious freedom is reassuring—and utterly at odds with the historical record. Wading into the controversy surrounding an Islamic center planned for a site near New York City's Ground Zero memorial this past August, President Obama declared:

"This is America. And our commitment to religious freedom must be unshakeable. The principle that people of all faiths are welcome in this country and that they will not be treated differently by their government is essential to who we are."

In doing so, he paid homage to a vision that politicians and preachers have extolled for more than two centuries—that America historically has been a place of religious tolerance. It was a sentiment George Washington voiced shortly after taking the oath of office just a few blocks from Ground Zero. But is it so?

In the storybook version most of us learned in school, the Pilgrims came to America aboard the Mayflower in search of religious freedom in 1620. The Puritans soon followed, for the same reason. Ever since these religious dissidents arrived at their shining "city upon a hill," as their governor John Winthrop called it, millions from around the world have done the same, coming to an America where they found a welcome melting pot in which everyone was free to practice his or her own faith.

The problem is that this tidy narrative is an American myth. The real story of religion in America's past is an often awkward, frequently embarrassing and occasionally bloody tale that most civics books and high-school texts either paper over or shunt to the side. And much of the recent conversation about America's ideal of religious freedom has paid lip service to this comforting tableau.

From the earliest arrival of Europeans on America's shores, religion has often been a cudgel, used to discriminate, suppress the foreign, the "heretic" and the "unbeliever"—including the "heathen" natives already here. Moreover, while the vast majority of early-generation Americans were Christian, the pitched battles between various Protestant sects and, more explosively, between Protestants and Catholics, present an unavoidable contradiction to the widely held notion that America is a "Christian nation." First, a little overlooked history: the initial encounter between Europeans in the future United States came with the establishment of a Huguenot (French Protestant) colony in 1564 at Fort Caroline (near modern Jacksonville, Florida).

More than half a century before the Mayflower set sail, French pilgrims had come to America in search of religious freedom. The Spanish had other ideas. In 1565, they established a forward operating base at St. Augustine and proceeded to wipe out the Fort Caroline colony. The Spanish commander, Pedro Menéndez de Aviles, wrote to the Spanish King Philip II that he had "hanged all those we had found in [Fort Caroline] because...they were scattering another Lutheran doctrine in these Provinces."

When hundreds of survivors of a shipwrecked French fleet washed up on the beaches of Florida, they were put to the sword, beside a river the Spanish called Matanzas ("slaughters").

In other words, the first encounter between European Christians in America ended in a blood bath. The much-ballyhooed arrival of the Pilgrims and Puritans in New England in the early 1600s was indeed a response to persecution that these religious dissenters had experienced in England.

According to, "Smithsonian Magazine by Kenneth C. Davis" October 2010, as the source. (America's True History of Religious Tolerance) The idea that the United States has always been a bastion of religious freedom is reassuring—and utterly at odds with the historical record. Wading into the controversy surrounding an Islamic center planned for a site near New York City's Ground Zero memorial this past August, President Obama declared:

"This is America. And our commitment to religious freedom must be unshakeable. The principle that people of all faiths are welcome in this country and that they will not be treated differently by their government is essential to who we are."

In doing so, he paid homage to a vision that politicians and preachers have extolled for more than two centuries—that America historically has been a place of religious tolerance. It was a sentiment George Washington voiced shortly after taking the oath of office just a few blocks from Ground Zero. But is it so?

In the storybook version most of us learned in school, the Pilgrims came to America aboard the Mayflower in search of religious freedom in 1620. The Puritans soon followed, for the same reason. Ever since these religious dissidents arrived at their shining "city upon a hill," as their governor John Winthrop called it, millions from around the world have done the same, coming to an America where they found a welcome melting pot in which everyone was free to practice his or her own faith.

The problem is that this tidy narrative is an American myth. The real story of religion in America's past is an often awkward, frequently embarrassing and occasionally bloody tale that most civics books and high-school texts either paper over or shunt to the side. And much of the recent conversation about America's ideal of religious freedom has paid lip service to this comforting tableau.

From the earliest arrival of Europeans on America's shores, religion has often been a cudgel, used to discriminate, suppress and even kill the foreign, the "heretic" and the "unbeliever"—including the "heathen" natives already here. Moreover, while it is true that the vast majority of early-generation Americans were Christian, the pitched battles between various Protestant sects and, more explosively, between Protestants and Catholics, present an unavoidable contradiction to the widely held notion that America is a "Christian nation." First, a little overlooked history: the initial encounter between Europeans in the future United States came with the establishment of a Huguenot (French Protestant) colony in 1564 at Fort Caroline (near modern Jacksonville, Florida).

More than half a century before the Mayflower set sail, French pilgrims had come to America in search of religious freedom. The Spanish had other ideas. In 1565, they established a forward operating base at St. Augustine and proceeded to wipe out the Fort Caroline colony. The Spanish commander, Pedro Menéndez de Avilés, wrote to the Spanish King Philip II that he had "hanged all those we had found in [Fort Caroline] because...they were scattering the odious Lutheran doctrine in these Provinces."

When hundreds of survivors of a shipwrecked French fleet washed up on the beaches of Florida, they were put to the sword, beside a river the Spanish called Matanzas ("slaughters").

In other words, the first encounter between European Christians in America ended in a blood bath. The much-ballyhooed arrival of the Pilgrims and Puritans in New England in the early 1600s was indeed a response to persecution that these religious dissenters had experienced in England.

In the book of John Hayah and the relationship to the India nation Bible printing. I remember a part of one side of my ancestor culture. The Indian often used the chant when praying for rain to the God. Hayah! Hayah! Hayah! the name of God was repeated as they prayed for rain.

In the book of the first English language Bible to be printed in America
Reference: The Cambridge world history of food. 2 (2000)

Published by the press syndicate of the University of Cambridge The Pitt building, Trumpington Street, Cambridge, United Kingdom

Cambridge University Press
The Edinburge Building, Cambridge CB2 2RU, UK
40 West 20th Street, New York, NY 10011-4211, USA
10 Scamford Road, Oakleigh, VIC 3166, Australia

Rulz de Alarcon 13, 28014 Madrid, Spain

Dock House, The Waterfront, Cape Town 8001, South Africia

http//www.Cambridge.org

A catalog record for this book is available from the British Library

Library of Congress Cataloging in Publication Data

The Cambridge world history of food / editions, Kenneth F. Kiple, Kriemhild Conet

TX353.C255 2000
641.309-dc21

ISBN O 521 40214 X (Volume 1)
ISBN O 521 40215 8 (Volume 2)
ISBN O 521 40216 6 (Set)

According to research found "WWW.GREATSITE. COM" as the resource. The Bibles of Colonial America, America's Earliest Bibles. In the early 1600's, the Geneva Bible became the first Bible to be taken across the Atlantic to America. It was, however, never printed in America. The first Bible printed in America was John Eliot's Algonquin Indian language Bible, which came off the press in 1663, and again in 1685. The Eliot Bible was in fact, the first Bible printed in the Western Hemisphere. American presses saw no other Bibles printed until well into the next century, when German emigrant Christopher Saur began production of the first European language Bibles printed in America: the German language Saur Bibles. The first edition of Saur's German Bible came off an American press in 1743. In 1763, Saur produced the first Bible printed on paper manufactured in America, and in 1776, Saur produced the first Bible printed from type manufactured in America… all of which were in the German language.

It was quite late in Colonial American history when the first English language Bible was printed in America, 1782 to be exact. Prior to this, English language Bibles were often available in the colonies, but they had to be imported from England. Not only was it financially more feasible to import English language Bibles rather than produce them, but there was also the legal issue of the fact that the "King James Version" of the Bible was still arguably the "copyright" of the English Crown, since "public domain" laws were not yet commonplace. Still, demand for Bibles was exceeding supply, particularly since England was keeping an import-export embargo against the rebellious colonists due to the Revolutionary War. American pride and independence was also on the line.

According to research found via "WWW.GREATSITE. COM" as the source. The fascinating story of how we got the Bible in its present form actually starts thousands of years ago, as briefly outlined in our Timeline of Bible Translation History. As a background study, we recommend that you first review our discussion of the Pre-Reformation History of the Bible from 1,400 B.C. to 1,400 A.D., which covers the transmission of the scripture through the original languages of Hebrew and Greek, and the 1,000 years of the Dark & Middle Ages when the Word was trapped in only Latin. Our starting point in this discussion of Bible history, however, is the advent of the scripture in the English language with the "Morning Star of the Reformation", John Wycliffe.

The first hand-written English language Bible manuscripts were produced in the 1380's AD by John Wycliffe, an Oxford professor, scholar, and theologian. Wycliffe, (also spelled "Wycliff" & "Wyclif"), was well-known throughout Europe for his opposition to the teaching of the organized Church, which he believed to be contrary to the Bible. With the help of his followers, called the Lollards, and his assistant Purvey, and many other faithful scribes, Wycliffe produced dozens of English language manuscript copies of the scriptures. They were translated out of the Latin Vulgate, which was the only source text available to Wycliffe. The Pope was so infuriated by his teachings and his translation of the Bible into English, that 44 years after Wycliffe had died, he ordered the bones to be dug-up, crushed, and scattered in the river!

One of Wycliffe's followers, John Hus, actively promoted Wycliffe's ideas: that people should be permitted to read the Bible in their own language, and they should oppose the tyranny of the Roman church that threatened anyone possessing a non-Latin Bible with execution. Hus was burned at the stake in 1415, with Wycliffe's manuscript Bibles used as kindling for the fire. The last words of John Hus were that, "in 100 years, God will raise up a man whose calls for reform cannot be suppressed." Almost exactly 100 years later, in 1517, Martin Luther nailed his famous 95 Theses of Contention (a list of 95 issues of heretical theology and crimes of the Roman Catholic Church) into the church door at Wittenberg. The prophecy of Hus had come true! Martin Luther went on to be the first person to translate and publish the Bible in the commonly-spoken dialect of the German people; a translation more appealing than previous German Biblical translations. Foxe's Book of Martyrs records that in that same year, 1517, seven people were burned at the stake by the Roman Catholic Church for the crime of teaching their children to say the Lord's Prayer in English rather than Latin.

Johann Gutenberg invented the printing press in the 1450's, and the first book to ever be printed was a Latin language

Bible, printed in Mainz, Germany. Gutenberg's Bibles were surprisingly beautiful, as each leaf Gutenberg printed was later colorfully hand-illuminated. Born as "Johann Gensfleisch" (John Gooseflesh), he preferred to be known as "Johann Gutenberg" (John Beautiful Mountain). Ironically, though he had created what many believe to be the most important invention in history, Gutenberg was a victim of unscrupulous business associates who took control of his business and left him in poverty. Nevertheless, the invention of the movable-type printing press meant that Bibles and books could finally be effectively produced in large quantities in a short period of time. This was essential to the success of the Reformation.

In the 1490's another Oxford professor, and the personal physician to King Henry the 7th and 8th, Thomas Linacre, decided to learn Greek. After reading the Gospels in Greek, and comparing it to the Latin Vulgate, he wrote in his diary, "Either this (the original Greek) is not the Gospel… or we are not Christians." The Latin had become so corrupt that it no longer even preserved the message of the Gospel… yet the Church still threatened to kill anyone who read the scripture in any language other than Latin… though Latin was not an original language of the scriptures.

In 1496, John Colet, another Oxford professor and the son of the Mayor of London, started reading the New Testament in Greek and translating it into English for his students at Oxford, and later for the public at Saint Paul's Cathedral in London. The people were so hungry to hear the Word of God in a language they could understand, that within six months there were 20,000 people packed in the church and at least that many outside trying to get in! (Sadly, while the enormous and beautiful Saint Paul's Cathedral remains the main church in London today, as of 2003, typical Sunday morning worship attendance is only around 200 people... and most of them are tourists). Fortunately for Colet, he was a powerful man with friends in high places, so he amazingly managed to avoid execution.

In considering the experiences of Linacre and Colet, the great scholar Erasmus was so moved to correct the corrupt Latin Vulgate, that in 1516, with the help of printer John Froben, he published a Greek-Latin Parallel New Testament. The Latin part was not the corrupt Vulgate, but his own fresh rendering of the text from the more accurate and reliable Greek, which he had managed to collate from a half-dozen partial old Greek New Testament manuscripts he had acquired. This milestone was the first non-Latin Vulgate text of the scripture to be produced in a millennium... and the first ever to come off a printing press. The 1516 Greek-Latin New Testament of Erasmus further focused attention on just how corrupt and inaccurate the Latin Vulgate had become, and how important it was to go back and use the original Greek (New Testament) and original Hebrew (Old Testament) languages to maintain accuracy... and to translate them faithfully into the languages of the common people, whether that be English, German, or any other tongue. No sympathy for this "illegal activity" was to be found from Rome... even as the words of Pope Leo X's declaration that "the fable of Christ was quite profitable to him" continued through the years to infuriate the people of God.

William Tyndale was the Captain of the Army of Reformers, and was their spiritual leader. Tyndale holds the distinction of being the first man to ever print the New Testament in the English language. Tyndale was a true scholar and a genius, so fluent in eight languages that it was said one would think any one of them to be his native tongue. He is frequently referred to as the "Architect of the English Language", (even more so than William Shakespeare) as so many of the phrases Tyndale coined are still in our language today.

Martin Luther had a small head-start on Tyndale, as Luther declared his intolerance for the Roman Church's corruption on Halloween in 1517, by nailing his 95 Theses of Contention to the Wittenberg Church door. Luther, who would be exiled in the months following the Diet of Worms Council in 1521 that was designed to martyr him, would translate the New Testament into German for the first time from the 1516 Greek-Latin New Testament of Erasmus, and publish it in September of 1522. Luther also published a German Pentateuch in 1523, and another edition of the German New Testament in 1529. In the 1530's he would go on to publish the entire Bible in German.

William Tyndale wanted to use the same 1516 Erasmus text as a source to translate and print the New Testament in English for the first time in history. Tyndale showed up on Luther's doorstep in Germany in 1525, and by year's end had translated the New Testament into English. Tyndale had been forced to flee England, because of the wide-spread rumor that his English New Testament project was underway, causing inquisitors and bounty hunters to be constantly on Tyndale's trail to arrest him and prevent his project. God foiled their plans, and in 1525-1526 the Tyndale New Testament became the first printed edition of the scripture in the English language. Subsequent printings of the Tyndale New Testament in the 1530's were often elaborately illustrated.

They were burned as soon as the Bishop could confiscate them, but copies trickled through and actually ended up in the bedroom of King Henry VIII. The more the King and Bishop resisted its distribution, the more fascinated the public at large became. The church declared it contained thousands of errors as they torched hundreds of New Testaments confiscated by the clergy, while in fact, they burned them because they could find no errors at all. One risked death by burning if caught in mere possession of Tyndale's forbidden books.

Having God's Word available to the public in the language of the common man, English, would have meant disaster to the church. No longer would they control access to the scriptures. If people were able to read the Bible in their own tongue, the church's income and power would crumble. They could not possibly continue to get away with selling indulgences (the forgiveness of sins) or selling the release of loved ones from a church-manufactured "Purgatory". People would begin to challenge the church's authority if the church were exposed as frauds and thieves. The contradictions between what God's Word said, and what the priests taught, would open the public's eyes and the truth would set them free from the grip of fear that the institutional church held. Salvation through faith, not works or donations, would be understood. The need for priests would vanish through the priesthood of all believers. The veneration of church-canonized Saints and Mary would be called into question. The availability of the scriptures in English was the biggest threat imaginable to the wicked church. Neither side would give up without a fight.

Today, there are only two known copies left of Tyndale's 1525-26 First Edition. Any copies printed prior to 1570 are extremely valuable. Tyndale's flight was an inspiration to freedom-loving Englishmen who drew courage from the 11 years that he was hunted. Books and Bibles flowed into England in bales of cotton and sacks of flour. Ironically, Tyndale's biggest customer was the King's men, who would buy up every copy available to burn them... and Tyndale used their money to print even more! In the end, Tyndale was caught: betrayed by an Englishman that he had befriended. Tyndale was incarcerated for 500 days before he was strangled and burned at the stake in 1536. Tyndale's last words were, "Oh Lord, open the King of England's eyes". This prayer would be answered just three years later in 1539, when King Henry VIII finally allowed, and even funded, the printing of an English Bible known as the "Great Bible". But before that could happen...

Myles Coverdale and John "Thomas Matthew" Rogers had remained loyal disciples the last six years of Tyndale's life, and they carried the English Bible project forward and even accelerated it. Coverdale finished translating the Old Testament, and in 1535 he printed the first complete Bible in the English language, making use of Luther's German text and the Latin as sources. Thus, the first complete English Bible was printed on October 4, 1535, and is known as the Coverdale Bible.

John Rogers went on to print the second complete English Bible in 1537. It was, however, the first English Bible translated from the original Biblical languages of Hebrew & Greek. He printed it under the pseudonym "Thomas Matthew", (an assumed name that had actually been used by Tyndale at one time) as a considerable part of this Bible was the translation of Tyndale, whose writings had been condemned by the English authorities. It is a composite made up of Tyndale's Pentateuch and New Testament (1534-1535 edition) and Coverdale's Bible and some of Roger's own translation of the text. It remains known most commonly as the Matthew-Tyndale Bible. It went through a nearly identical second-edition printing in 1549.

In 1539, Thomas Cranmer, the Archbishop of Canterbury, hired Myles Coverdale at the bequest of King Henry VIII to publish the "Great Bible". It became the first English Bible authorized for public use, as it was distributed to every church, chained to the pulpit, and a reader was even provided so that the illiterate could hear the Word of God in plain English. It would seem that William Tyndale's last wish had been granted...just three years after his martyrdom. Cranmer's Bible, published by Coverdale, was known as the Great Bible due to its great size: a large pulpit folio measuring over 14 inches tall. Seven editions of this version were printed between April of 1539 and December of 1541.

It was not that King Henry VIII had a change of conscience regarding publishing the Bible in English. His motives were more sinister… but the Lord sometimes uses the evil intentions of men to bring about His glory. King Henry VIII had in fact, requested that the Pope permit him to divorce his wife and marry his mistress. The Pope refused. King Henry responded by marrying his mistress anyway, (later having two of his many wives executed), and thumbing his nose at the Pope by renouncing Roman Catholicism, taking England out from under Rome's religious control, and declaring himself as the reigning head of State to also be the new head of the Church. This new branch of the Christian Church, neither Roman Catholic nor truly Protestant, became known as the Anglican Church or the Church of England. King Henry acted essentially as its "Pope". His first act was to further defy the wishes of Rome by funding the printing of the scriptures in English… the first legal English Bible… just for spite.

The ebb and flow of freedom continued through the 1540's… and into the 1550's. After King Henry VIII, King Edward VI took the throne, and after his death, the reign of Queen "Bloody" Mary was the next obstacle to the printing of the Bible in English. She was possessed in her quest to return England to the Roman Church. In 1555, John "Thomas Matthew" Rogers and Thomas Cranmer were both burned at the stake. Mary went on to burn reformers at the stake by the hundreds for the "crime" of being a Protestant. This era was known as the Marian Exile, and the refugees fled from

England with little hope of ever seeing their home or friends again.

In the 1550's, the Church at Geneva, Switzerland, was very sympathetic to the reformer refugees and was one of only a few safe havens for a desperate people. Many of them met in Geneva, led by Myles Coverdale and John Foxe (publisher of the famous Foxe's Book of Martyrs, which is to this day the only exhaustive reference work on the persecution and martyrdom of Early Christians and Protestants from the first century up to the mid-16th century), as well as Thomas Sampson and William Whittingham. There, with the protection of the great theologian John Calvin (author of the most famous theological book ever published, Calvin's Institutes of the Christian Religion) and John Knox, the great Reformer of the Scottish Church, the Church of Geneva determined to produce a Bible that would educate their families while they continued in exile.

The New Testament was completed in 1557, and the complete Bible was first published in 1560. It became known as the Geneva Bible. Due to a passage in Genesis describing the clothing that God fashioned for Adam and Eve upon expulsion from the Garden of Eden as "Breeches" (an antiquated form of "Britches"), some people referred to the Geneva Bible as the Breeches Bible.

The Geneva Bible was the first Bible to add numbered verses to the chapters, so that referencing specific passages would be easier. Every chapter was also accompanied by extensive marginal notes and references so thorough and complete that the Geneva Bible is also considered the first English "Study Bible". William Shakespeare quotes hundreds of times in his plays from the Geneva translation of the Bible. The Geneva Bible became the Bible of choice for over 100 years of English speaking Christians. Between 1560 and 1644 at least 144 editions of this Bible were published. Examination of the 1611 King James Bible shows clearly that its translators were influenced much more by the Geneva Bible, than by any other source. The Geneva Bible itself retains over 90% of William Tyndale's original English translation. The Geneva in fact, remained more popular than the King James Version until decades after its original release in 1611! The Geneva holds the honor of being the first Bible taken to America, and the Bible of the Puritans and Pilgrims. It is truly the "Bible of the Protestant Reformation." Strangely, the famous Geneva Bible has been out-of-print since 1644, so the only way to obtain one is to either purchase an original printing of the Geneva Bible, or a less costly facsimile reproduction of the original 1560 Geneva Bible.

With the end of Queen Mary's bloody reign, the reformers could safely return to England. The Anglican Church, now under Queen Elizabeth I, reluctantly tolerated the printing and distribution of Geneva version Bibles in England. The marginal notes, which were vehemently against the institutional Church of the day, did not rest well with the rulers of the day. Another version, one with a less inflammatory tone was desired, and the copies of the Great Bible were getting to be decades old. In 1568, a revision of the Great Bible known as the Bishop's Bible was introduced. Despite 19 editions being printed between 1568 and 1606, this Bible, referred to as the "rough draft of the King James Version", never gained much of a foothold of popularity among the people. The Geneva may have simply been too much to compete with.

By the 1580's, the Roman Catholic Church saw that it had lost the battle to suppress the will of God: that His Holy Word be available in the English language. In 1582, the Church of Rome surrendered their fight for "Latin only" and decided that if the Bible was to be available in English, they would at least have an official Roman Catholic English translation. And so, using the corrupt and inaccurate Latin Vulgate as the only source text, they went on to publish an English Bible with all the distortions and corruptions that Erasmus had revealed and warned of 75 years earlier. Because it was translated at the Roman Catholic College in the city of Rheims, it was known as the Rheims New Testament (also spelled Rhemes). The Douay Old Testament was translated by the Church of Rome in 1609 at the College in the city of Douay (also spelled Doway & Douai). The combined product is commonly referred to as the "Doway/Rheims" Version. In 1589, Dr. William Fulke of Cambridge published the "Fulke's Refutation", in which he printed in parallel columns the Bishops Version along side the Rheims Version, attempting to show the error and distortion of the Roman Church's corrupt compromise of an English version of the Bible.

With the death of Queen Elizabeth I, Prince James VI of Scotland became King James I of England. The Protestant clergy approached the new King in 1604 and announced their desire for a new translation to replace the Bishop's Bible first printed in 1568. They knew that the Geneva Version had won the hearts of the people because of its excellent scholarship, accuracy, and exhaustive commentary. However, they did not want the controversial marginal notes (proclaiming the Pope an Anti-Christ, etc.) Essentially, the leaders of the church desired a Bible for the people, with scriptural references only for word clarification or cross-references.

This "translation to end all translations" (for a while at least) was the result of the combined effort of about fifty scholars. They took into consideration: The Tyndale New Testament, The Coverdale Bible, The Matthews Bible, The Great Bible, The Geneva Bible, and even the Rheims New Testament.

The great revision of the Bishop's Bible had begun. From 1605 to 1606 the scholars engaged in private research. From 1607 to 1609 the work was assembled. In 1610 the work went to press, and in 1611 the first of the huge (16 inch tall) pulpit folios known today as "The 1611 King James Bible" came off the printing press. A typographical discrepancy in Ruth 3:15 rendered a pronoun "He" instead of "She" in that verse in some printings. This caused some of the 1611 First Editions to be known by collectors as "He" Bibles, and others as "She" Bibles. Starting just one year after the huge 1611 pulpit-size King James Bibles were printed and chained to every church pulpit in England; printing then began on the earliest normal-size printings of the King James Bible. These were produced so individuals could have their own personal copy of the Bible.

The Anglican Church's King James Bible took decades to overcome the more popular Protestant Church's Geneva Bible. One of the greatest ironies of history, is that many Protestant Christian churches today embrace the King James Bible exclusively as the "only" legitimate English language translation... yet it is not even a Protestant translation! It was printed to compete with the Protestant Geneva Bible, by authorities who throughout most of history were hostile to Protestants... and killed them. While many Protestants are quick to assign the full blame of persecution to the Roman

Catholic Church, it should be noted that even after England broke from Roman Catholicism in the 1500's, the Church of England (The Anglican Church) continued to persecute Protestants throughout the 1600's. One famous example of this is John Bunyan, who while in prison for the crime of preaching the Gospel, wrote one of Christian history's greatest books, Pilgrim's Progress. Throughout the 1600's, as the Puritans and the Pilgrims fled the religious persecution of England to cross the Atlantic and start a new free nation in America, they took with them their precious Geneva Bible, and rejected the King's Bible. America was founded upon the Geneva Bible, not the King James Bible.

Protestants today are largely unaware of their own history, and unaware of the Geneva Bible (which is textually 95% the same as the King James Version, but 50 years older than the King James Version, and not influenced by the Roman Catholic Rheims New Testament that the King James translators admittedly took into consideration). Nevertheless, the King James Bible turned out to be an excellent and accurate translation, and it became the most printed book in the history of the world, and the only book with one billion copies in print. In fact, for over 250 years...until the appearance of the English Revised Version of 1881-1885... the King James Version reigned without much of a rival. One little-known fact, is that for the past 200 years, all King James

Bibles published in America are actually the 1769 Baskerville spelling and wording revision of the 1611. The original "1611" preface is deceivingly included by the publishers, and no mention of the fact that it is really the 1769 version is to be found, because that might hurt sales. The only way to obtain a true, unaltered, 1611 version is to either purchase an original pre-1769 printing of the King James Bible, or a less costly facsimile reproduction of the original 1611 King James Bible.

Although the first Bible printed in America was done in the native Algonquin Indian Language by John Eliot in 1663; the first English language Bible to be printed in America by Robert Aitken in 1782 was a King James Version. Robert Aitken's 1782 Bible was also the only Bible ever authorized by the United States Congress. He was commended by President George Washington for providing Americans with Bibles during the embargo of imported English goods due to the Revolutionary War. In 1808, Robert's daughter, Jane Aitken, would become the first woman to ever print a Bible… and to do so in America, of course. In 1791, Isaac Collins vastly improved upon the quality and size of the typesetting of American Bibles and produced the first "Family Bible" printed in America… also a King James Version. Also in 1791, Isaiah Thomas published the first Illustrated Bible printed in America…in the King James Version. For more information on the earliest Bibles printed in America from the 1600's through the early 1800's, you may wish to review our more detailed discussion of The Bibles of Colonial America.

While Noah Webster, just a few years after producing his famous Dictionary of the English Language, would produce his own modern translation of the English Bible in 1833; the public remained too loyal to the King James Version for Webster's version to have much impact. It was not really until the 1880's that England's own planned replacement for their King James Bible, the English Revised Version(E.R.V.) would become the first English language Bible to gain popular acceptance as a post-King James Version modern-English Bible. The widespread popularity of this modern-English translation brought with it another curious characteristic: the absence of the 14 Apocryphal books.

Up until the 1880's every Protestant Bible (not just Catholic Bibles) had 80 books, not 66! The inter-testamental books written hundreds of years before Christ called "The Apocrypha" were part of virtually every printing of the Tyndale-Matthews Bible, the Great Bible, the Bishops Bible, the Protestant Geneva Bible, and the King James Bible until their removal in the 1880's! The original 1611 King James contained the Apocrypha, and King James threatened anyone who dared to print the Bible without the Apocrypha with heavy fines and a year in jail. Only for the last 120 years has the Protestant Church rejected these books, and removed them from their Bibles. This has left most modern-day Christians believing the popular myth that there is something "Roman Catholic" about the Apocrypha. There is, however, no truth in that myth, and no widely-accepted reason for the removal of the Apocrypha in the 1880's has ever been officially issued by a mainline Protestant denomination.

The Americans responded to England's E.R.V. Bible by publishing the nearly-identical American Standard Version (A.S.V.) in 1901. It was also widely-accepted and embraced by churches throughout America for many decades as the leading modern-English version of the Bible. In the 1971, it was again revised and called New American Standard Version Bible (often referred to as the N.A.S.V. or N.A.S.B. or N.A.S.). This New American Standard Bible is considered by nearly all evangelical Christian scholars and translators today, to be the most accurate, word-for-word translation of the original Greek and Hebrew scriptures into the modern English language that has ever been produced. It remains the most popular version among theologians, professors, scholars, and seminary students today. Some, however, have taken issue with it because it is so direct and literal a translation (focused on accuracy), that it does not flow as easily in conversational English.

For this reason, in 1973, the New International Version (N.I.V.) was produced, which was offered as a "dynamic equivalent" translation into modern English. The N.I.V. was designed not for "word-for-word" accuracy, but rather, for "phrase-for-phrase" accuracy, and ease of reading even at a Junior High-School reading level. It was meant to appeal to a broader (and in some instances less-educated) cross-section of the general public. Critics of the N.I.V. often jokingly refer to it as the "Nearly Inspired Version", but that has not stopped it from becoming the best-selling modern-English translation of the Bible ever published.

In 1982, Thomas Nelson Publishers produced what they called the "New King James Version". Their original intent was to keep the basic wording of the King James to appeal to King James Version loyalists, while only changing the most obscure words and the Elizabethan "thee, thy, thou" pronouns. This was an interesting marketing ploy, however, upon discovering that this was not enough of a change for them to be able to legally copyright the result, they had to make more significant revisions, which defeated their purpose in the first place. It was never taken seriously by scholars, but it has enjoyed some degree of public acceptance, simply because of its clever "New King James Version" marketing name.

In 2002, a major attempt was made to bridge the gap between the simple readability of the N.I.V., and the extremely precise accuracy of the N.A.S.B. This translation is called the English Standard Version (E.S.V.) and is rapidly gaining popularity for its readability and accuracy. The 21st Century will certainly continue to bring new translations of God's Word in the modern English language.

As Christians, we must be very careful to make intelligent and informed decisions about what translations of the Bible we choose to read. On the liberal extreme, we have people who would give us heretical new translations that attempt to change God's Word to make it politically correct. One example of this, which has made headlines recently is the Today's New International Version (T.N.I.V.) which seeks to remove all gender-specific references in the Bible whenever possible! Not all new translations are good... and some are very bad.

But equally dangerous, is the other extreme... of blindly rejecting ANY English translation that was produced in the four centuries that have come after the 1611 King James. We must remember that the main purpose of the Protestant Reformation was to get the Bible out of the chains of being trapped in an ancient language that few could understand, and into the modern, spoken, conversational language of the present day. William Tyndale fought and died for the right to print the Bible in the common, spoken, modern English tongue of his day... as he boldly told one official who criticized his efforts, "If God spare my life, I will see to it that the boy who drives the plowshare knows more of the scripture than you, Sir!"

Will we now go backwards, and seek to imprison God's Word once again exclusively in ancient translations? Clearly it is not God's will that we over-react to SOME of the bad modern translations, by rejecting ALL new translations and "throwing the baby out with the bathwater". The Word of God is unchanging from generation to generation, but language is a dynamic and ever-changing form of communication. We therefore have a responsibility before God as Christians to make sure that each generation has a modern translation that they can easily understand, yet that does not sacrifice accuracy in any way. Let's be ever mindful that we are not called to worship the Bible. That is called idolatry. We are called to worship the God who gave us the Bible, and who preserved it through the centuries of people who sought to destroy it.

The Pre-Reformation History of the Bible From 1,400 BC to 1,400 AD

The story of how we got the English language Bible is, for the most part, the story of the Protestant Reformation which began in the late 14th Century AD with John Wycliffe. Indeed, if we go back more than just one thousand years, there is no language recognizable as "English" that even existed anywhere. The story of the Bible is much older than that, however.

The first recorded instance of God's Word being written down, was when the Lord Himself wrote it down in the form of ten commandments on the stone tablets delivered to Moses at the top of Mount Sinai. Biblical scholars believe this occurred between **1,400 BC** and **1,500 BC**… almost 3,500 years ago. The language used was almost certainly an ancient form of Hebrew, the language of Old Covenant believers.

The earliest scripture is generally considered to be the "Pentateuch", the first five books of the Moses: Genesis, Exodus, Leviticus, Numbers, & Deuteronomy… though there is some scholarly evidence to indicate that the Old Testament Book of Job may actually be the oldest book in the Bible. The Old Testament scriptures were written in ancient Hebrew, a language substantially different than the Hebrew of today. These writings were passed down from generation to generation for thousands of years on scrolls made of animal skin, usually sheep, but sometimes deer or cow. Animals considered "unclean" by the Jews, such as pigs, were of course, never used to make scrolls.

When the entire Pentateuch is present on a scroll, it is called a "Torah". An entire Torah Scroll, if completely unraveled, is over 150 feet long! As most sheep are only about two to three feet long, it took an entire flock of sheep to make just one Torah scroll. The Jewish scribes who painstakingly produced each scroll were perfectionists. If they made even the slightest mistake in copying, such as allowing two letters of a word to touch, they destroyed that entire panel (the last three or four columns of text), and the panel before it, because it had touched the panel with a mistake! While most Christians today would consider this behavior fanatical and even idolatrous (worshiping the scripture, rather than the One who gave it to us), it nevertheless demonstrates the level of faithfulness to accuracy applied to the preservation of God's Word throughout the first couple of thousand years of Biblical transmission.

Hebrew has one thing in common with English: they are both "picture languages". Their words form a clear picture in your mind. As evidence of this; the first man to ever print the scriptures in English, William Tyndale, once commented that Hebrew was ten times easier to translate into English than any other language. Tyndale would certainly be qualified to make such a statement, as he was so fluent in eight languages, that it was said you would have thought any one of them to be his native tongue.

By approximately **500 BC**, the 39 Books that make up the Old Testament were completed, and continued to be preserved in Hebrew on scrolls. As we approach the last few centuries before Christ, the Jewish historical books known as the "Apocrypha" were completed, yet they were recorded in Greek rather than Hebrew. By the end of the **First Century AD**, the New Testament had been completed. It was preserved in Greek on Papyrus, a thin paper-like material made from crushed and flattened stalks of a reed-like plant. The word "Bible" comes from the same Greek root word as "papyrus". The papyrus sheets were bound, or tied together in a configuration much more similar to modern books than to an elongated scroll.

These groupings of papyrus were called a "codex" (plural: "codices"). The oldest copies of the New Testament known to exist today are: The Codex Alexandrius and the Codex Sinaiticus in the British Museum Library in London, and the Codex Vaticanus in the Vatican. They date back to approximately the **300's AD**. In **315 AD**, Athenasius, the Bishop of Alexandria, identified the 27 Books which we recognize today as the canon of New Testament scripture.

In **382 AD**, the early church father Jerome translated the New Testament from its original Greek into Latin. This translation became known as the "Latin Vulgate", ("Vulgate" meaning "vulgar" or "common"). He put a note next to the Apocrypha Books, stating that he did not know whether or not they were inspired scripture, or just Jewish historical writings which accompanied the Old Testament.

The Apocrypha was kept as part of virtually every Bible scribed or printed from these early days until just 120 years ago, in the mid-1880's, when it was removed from Protestant Bibles. Up until the 1880's, however, every Christian… Protestant or otherwise… embraced the Apocrypha as part of the Bible, though debate continued as to whether or not the Apocrypha was inspired. There is no truth to the popular myth that there is something "Roman Catholic" about the Apocrypha, which stemmed from the fact that the Roman Catholics kept 12 of the 14 Apocrypha Books in their Bible, as the Protestants removed all of them. No real justification was ever given for the removal of these ancient Jewish writings from before the time of Christ, which had remained untouched and part of every Bible for nearly two thousand years.

By **500 AD** the Bible had been translated into over 500 languages. Just one century later, by **600 AD**, it has been restricted to only one language: the Latin Vulgate! The only organized and recognized church at that time in history was the Catholic Church of Rome, and they refused to allow the scripture to be available in any language other than Latin. Those in possession of non-Latin scriptures would be executed! This was because only the priests were educated to understand Latin, and this gave the church ultimate power… a power to rule without question… a power to deceive… a power to extort money from the masses. Nobody could question their "Biblical" teachings, because few people other than priests could read Latin. The church capitalized on this forced-ignorance through the 1,000 year period from 400 AD to 1,400 AD knows as the "Dark and Middle Ages".

Pope Leo the Tenth established a practice called the "selling of indulgences" as a way to extort money from the people. He offered forgiveness of sins for a fairly small amount of money. For a little bit more money, you would be allowed to indulge in a continuous lifestyle of sin, such as keeping a mistress. Also, through the invention of "Purgatory", you could purchase the salvation of your loved-one's souls. The church taught the ignorant masses, *"As soon as the coin in the coffer rings, the troubled soul from Purgatory springs!"* Pope Leo the Tenth showed his true feelings when he said, *"The fable of Christ has been quite profitable to us!"*

Editorial Note: Let us state at this point, that it is not our intent to offend or "bash" Roman Catholics. It is unavoidable that every historical account has its "good guys" and its "bad guys". Just as it is impossible to accurately tell the story of World War Two without offending the Germans and the Italians who were undeniably the enemies of world peace at that time… it is equally impossible to accurately tell the story of the English Bible without unintentionally offending those who continue to revere the Roman Catholic and Anglican Churches.

Where was the true church of God during these Dark Ages?

On the Scottish Island of Iona, in **563 AD**, a man named Columba started a Bible College. For the next 700 years, this was the source of much of the non-Catholic, evangelical Bible teaching through those centuries of the Dark and Middle Ages. The students of this college were called "Culdees", which means "certain stranger". The Culdees were a secret society, and the remnant of the true Christian faith was kept alive by these men during the many centuries that led up to the Protestant Reformation.

In fact, the first man to be called a "Culdee" was Joseph of Aremethia. The Bible tells us that Joseph of Aremethia gave up his tomb for Jesus. Tradition tells us that he was actually the Uncle of the Virgin Mary, and therefore the Great-Uncle (or "half-Uncle" at least) of Jesus. It is also believed that Joseph of Aremethia traveled to the British Isles shortly after the resurrection of Christ, and built the first Christian Church above ground there. Tradition also tells us that Jesus may have spent much of his young adult life (between 13 and 30) traveling the world with his Great Uncle Joseph… though the Bible is silent on these years in the life of Jesus.

In the late 1300's, the secret society of Culdees chose <u>John Wycliffe</u> to lead the world out of the Dark Ages. Wycliffe has been called the "Morning Star of the Reformation". That Protestant Reformation was about one thing: getting the Word of God back into the hands of the masses in their own native language, so that the corrupt church would be exposed and the message of salvation in Christ alone, by scripture alone, through faith alone would be proclaimed again.

We are also called to preserve the ancient, original English translations of the Bible… and that is what we do here at According to <u>WWW.GREATSITE.COM</u>" as the source. Consider the following textual comparison of the earliest English translations of John 3:16, as shown in the English Hexapla Parallel New Testament:

1st Ed. King James (1611): "For God so loued the world, that he gaue his only begotten Sonne: that whosoeuer beleeueth in him, should not perish, but haue euerlasting life."

Rheims (1582): "For so God loued the vvorld, that he gaue his only-begotten sonne: that euery one that beleeueth in him, perish not, but may haue life euerlasting"

Geneva (1560): "For God so loueth the world, that he hath geuen his only begotten Sonne: that none that beleue in him, should peryshe, but haue euerlasting lyfe."

Great Bible (1539): "For God so loued the worlde, that he gaue his only begotten sonne, that whosoeuer beleueth in him, shulde not perisshe, but haue euerlasting lyfe."

Tyndale (1534): "For God so loveth the worlde, that he hath geven his only sonne, that none that beleve in him, shuld perisshe: but shuld have everlastinge lyfe."

Wycliff (1380): "for god loued so the world; that he gaf his oon bigetun sone, that eche man that bileueth in him perisch not: but haue euerlastynge liif,"

Anglo-Saxon Proto-English Manuscripts (995 AD): "God lufode middan-eard swa, dat he seade his an-cennedan sunu, dat nan ne forweorde de on hine gely ac habbe dat ece lif."

Timeline of Bible Translation History

1,400 BC: The first written Word of God: The Ten Commandments delivered to Moses.

500 BC: Completion of All Original Hebrew Manuscripts which make up The 39 Books of the Old Testament.

200 BC: Completion of the Septuagint Greek Manuscripts which contain The 39 Old Testament Books AND 14 Apocrypha Books.

1st Century AD: Completion of All Original Greek Manuscripts which make up The 27 Books of the New Testament.

315 AD: Athenasius, the Bishop of Alexandria, identifies the 27 books of the New Testament which are today recognized as the canon of scripture.

382 AD: Jerome's Latin Vulgate Manuscripts Produced which contain All 80 Books (39 Old Test. + 14 Apocrypha + 27 New Test).

500 AD: Scriptures have been Translated into Over 500 Languages.

600 AD: LATIN was the Only Language Allowed for Scripture.

995 AD: Anglo-Saxon (Early Roots of English Language) Translations of The New Testament Produced.

1384 AD: Wycliffe is the First Person to Produce a (Hand-Written) manuscript Copy of the Complete Bible; All 80 Books.

1455 AD: Gutenberg Invents the Printing Press; Books May Now be mass-Produced Instead of Individually Hand-Written. The First Book Ever Printed is Gutenberg's Bible in Latin.

1516 AD: Erasmus Produces a Greek/Latin Parallel New Testament.

1522 AD: Martin Luther's German New Testament.

1526 AD: William Tyndale's New Testament; The First New Testament printed in the English Language.

1535 AD: Myles Coverdale's Bible; The First Complete Bible printed in the English Language (80 Books: O.T. & N.T. & Apocrypha).

1537 AD: Tyndale-Matthews Bible; The Second Complete Bible printed in English. Done by John "Thomas Matthew" Rogers (80 Books).

1539 AD: The "Great Bible" Printed; The First English Language Bible Authorized for Public Use (80 Books).

1560 AD: The Geneva Bible Printed; The First English Language Bible to add Numbered Verses to Each Chapter (80 Books).

1568 AD: The Bishops Bible Printed; The Bible of which the King James was a Revision (80 Books).

1609 AD: The Douay Old Testament is added to the Rheims New Testament (of 1582) Making the First Complete English Catholic Bible; Translated from the Latin Vulgate (80 Books).

1611 AD: The King James Bible Printed; Originally with All 80 Books. The Apocrypha was Officially Removed in 1885 Leaving Only 66 Books.

1782 AD: Robert Aitken's Bible; The First English Language Bible (KJV) Printed in America.

1791 AD: Isaac Collins and Isaiah Thomas Respectively Produce the First Family Bible and First Illustrated Bible Printed in America. Both were King James Versions, with All 80 Books.

1808 AD: Jane Aitken's Bible (Daughter of Robert Aitken); The First Bible to be Printed by a Woman.

1833 AD: Noah Webster's Bible; After Producing his Famous Dictionary, Webster Printed his Own Revision of the King James Bible.

1841 AD: English Hexapla New Testament; an Early Textual Comparison showing the Greek and 6 Famous English Translations in Parallel Columns.

1846 AD: The Illuminated Bible; The Most Lavishly Illustrated Bible printed in America. A King James Version, with All 80 Books.

1863 AD: Robert Young's "Literal" Translation; often criticized for being so literal that it sometimes obscures the contextual English meaning.

1885 AD: The "English Revised Version" Bible; The First Major English Revision of the KJV.

1901 AD: The "American Standard Version"; The First Major American Revision of the KJV.

1952 AD: The "Revised Standard Version" (RSV); said to be a Revision of the 1901 American Standard Version, though more highly criticized.

1971 AD: The "New American Standard Bible" (NASB) is Published as a "Modern and Accurate Word for Word English Translation" of the Bible.

1973 AD: The "New International Version" (NIV) is Published as a "Modern and Accurate Phrase for Phrase English Translation" of the Bible.

1982 AD: The "New King James Version" (NKJV) is Published as a "Modern English Version Maintaining the Original Style of the King James."

1990 AD: The "New Revised Standard Version" (NRSV); further revision of 1952 RSV, (itself a revision of 1901 ASV), criticized for "gender inclusiveness".

2002 AD: The English Standard Version (ESV) is published as a translation to bridge the gap between the accuracy of the NASB and the readability of the NIV.

Matthew 7:7-8 and 11:28 — "...Seek and you will find;... he who seeks finds...Come to me...and I will give you rest." Pap. Ox. 654.5-9 — (Jesus says:) 'Let him who seek(s) not cease (seeking until) he finds; and when he find (he will) be astonished, and having (astoun) ded, he will reign; an (d reigning), he will (re)st' (Clement of Alexandria also knows the saying in this form.) Gospel of Thomas 2 — 'Jesus said: He who seeks should not stop seeking until he finds; and when he finds, he will be bewildered (beside himself); and when he is bewildered he will marvel, and will reign over the All.'41

Christ said: He who seeks should not stop seeking until he finds; and when he finds, he will be bewildered (beside himself); and when he is bewildered he will marvel, and will reign over the All.

'According to my experience Willie Stanfield, with talking to other religion's, Some Christians say the rapture that some believe is not where Christ will take the church. They believe it is the END of those who are taken and the left behind are those who will enter into the Tribulation as the church.

'I Willie Stanfield has reviewed and understands the scripture of end times, according to the King James book of Matthew 21:23-46: States,'

23. And when he was come into the temple, the chief priests and the elders of the people came unto him as he was teaching, and said, By what authority doest thou these things? and who gave thee this authority?

24. And Jesus answered and said unto them, I also will ask you one thing, which if ye tell me, I in likewise will tell you by what authority I do these things.

25. The baptism of John, whence was it? From heaven, or of men? And they reasoned with themselves, saying, If we shall say, From heaven; he will say unto us, Why did ye not then believe him?

26. But if we shall say, Of men; we fear the people; for all hold John as a prophet.

27. And they answered Jesus, and said, We cannot tell. And he said unto them, Neither tell I you by what authority I do these things.

28. But what think ye? A certain man had two sons; and he came to the first, and said, Son, go work today in my vineyard.

29. He answered and said, I will not: but afterward he repented, and went.

30. And he came to the second, and said likewise. And he answered and said, I go, sir: and went not.

31. Whether of them twain did the will of God? They say unto him, The first. Jesus saith unto them, Verily I say unto you, That the publicans and the harlots go into the kingdom of God before you.

32. For John came unto you in the way of righteousness, and ye believed him not: but the publicans and the harlots believed him: and ye, when ye had seen it, repented not afterward, that ye might believe him.

33. Hear another parable: There was a certain householder, which planted a vineyard, and hedged it round about, and digged a winepress in it, and built a tower, and let it out to husbandmen, and went into a far country:

34. And when the time of the fruit drew near, he sent his servants to the husbandmen, that they might receive the fruits of it.

35. And the husbandmen took his servants, and beat one, and killed another, and stoned another.

36. Again, he sent other servants more than the first: and they did unto them likewise.

37. But last of all he sent unto them his son, saying, They will reverence my son.

38. But when the husbandmen saw the son, they said among themselves, This is the heir; come, let us kill him, and let us seize on his inheritance.

39. And they caught him, and cast him out of the vineyard, and slew him.

40. When the lord therefore of the vineyard cometh, what will he do unto those husbandmen?

41. They say unto him, He will miserably destroy those wicked men, and will let out his vineyard unto other husbandmen, which shall render him the fruits in their seasons.

42. Jesus saith unto them, Did ye never read in the scriptures, The stone which the builders rejected, the same is become the head of the corner: this is the Lord's doing, and it is marvellous in our eyes?

43. Therefore say I unto you, The kingdom of God shall be taken from you, and given to a nation bringing forth the fruits thereof.

44. And whosoever shall fall on this stone shall be broken: but on whomsoever it shall fall, it will grind him to powder.

45. And when the chief priests and Pharisees had heard his parables, they perceived that he spake of them.

46. But when they sought to lay hands on him, they feared the multitude, because they took him for a prophet.

'And to Show that the Kingdom of God was taken from the Jews and given to the Genitals. They were added to the Kingdom of God and ever Peter doubted before hand and had to believe himself.'

Joel 2:28-32; John 14:15-26; John 16:5-16; Acts 2:1-13; Acts 19:1-7

Peter Summoned to Caesarea -17Now while Peter doubted in himself what this vision which he had seen should mean, behold, the men which were sent from Cornelius had made inquiry for Simon's house, and stood before the gate, 18And called, and asked whether Simon, which was surnamed Peter, were lodged there. 19While Peter thought on the vision, the Spirit said unto him, Behold, three men seek thee. 20Arise therefore, and get thee down, and go with them, doubting nothing: for I have sent them. 21Then Peter went down to the men which were sent unto him from Cornelius; and said, Behold, I am he whom ye seek: what is the cause wherefore ye are come? 22And they said, Cornelius the centurion, a just man, and one that feareth God, and of good report among all the nation of the Jews, was warned from God by an holy angel to send for thee into his house, and to hear words of thee. 23Then called he them in, and lodged them. And on the morrow Peter went away with them, and certain brethren from Joppa accompanied him.

34Then Peter opened his mouth, and said, of a truth I perceive that God is no respecter of persons: 35But in every nation he that feareth him, and worketh righteousness, is accepted with him. 36The word which God sent unto the children of Israel, preaching peace by Jesus Christ: (he is Lord of all:) 37That word, I say, ye know, which was published throughout all Judaea, and began from Galilee, after the baptism which John preached; 38How God anointed Jesus of Nazareth with the Holy Ghost and with power: who went about doing good, and healing all that were oppressed of the devil; for God was with him. 39And we are witnesses of all things which he did both in the land of the Jews, and in Jerusalem; whom they slew and hanged on a tree: 40Him God raised up the third day, and shewed him openly; 41Not to all the people, but unto witnesses chosen before of God, even to us, who did eat and drink with him after he rose from the dead. 42And he commanded us to preach unto the people, and to testify that it is he which was ordained of God to be the Judge of quick and dead. 43To him give all the prophets witness, that through his name whosoever believeth in him shall receive remission of sins.

44While Peter yet spake these words, the Holy Ghost fell on all them which heard the word. 45And they of the circumcision which believed were astonished, as many as came with Peter, because that on the Gentiles also was poured out the gift of the Holy Ghost. 46For they heard them speak with tongues, and magnify God. Then answered Peter, 47Can any man forbid water, that these should not be baptized, which have received the Holy Ghost as well as we? 48And he commanded them to be baptized in the name of the Lord. Then prayed they him to tarry certain days.

Galatians 3:10-28 -10For as many as are of the works of the law are under the curse: for it is written, Cursed is every one that continueth not in all things which are written in the book of the law to do them. 11But that no man is justified by the law in the sight of God, it is evident: for, The just shall live by faith. 12And the law is not of faith: but, The man that doeth them shall live in them. 13Christ hath redeemed us from the curse of the law, being made a curse for us: for it is written, Cursed is every one that hangeth on a tree: 14That the blessing of Abraham might come on the Gentiles through Jesus Christ; that we might receive the promise of the Spirit through faith.

The Purpose of the Law-15Brethren, I speak after the manner of men; Though it be but a man's covenant, yet if it be confirmed, no man disannulleth, or addeth thereto. 16Now to Abraham and his seed were the promises made. He saith not, And to seeds, as of many; but as of one, And to thy seed, which is Christ. 17And this I say, that the covenant, that was confirmed before of God in Christ, the law, which was four hundred and thirty years after, cannot disannul, that it should make the promise of none effect. 18For if the inheritance be of the law, it is no more of promise: but God gave it to Abraham by promise.

19Wherefore then serveth the law? It was added because of transgressions, till the seed should come to whom the promise was made; and it was ordained by angels in the hand of a mediator. 20Now a mediator is not a mediator of one, but God is one. 21Is the law then against the promises of God? God forbid: for if there had been a law given which could have given life, verily righteousness should have been by the law. 22But the scripture hath concluded all under sin, that the promise by faith of Jesus Christ might be given to them that believe.

23But before faith came, we were kept under the law, shut up unto the faith which should afterwards be revealed. 24Wherefore the law was our schoolmaster to bring us unto Christ, that we might be justified by faith. 25But after that faith is come, we are no longer under a schoolmaster.

Sons Through Faith in Christ - 26For ye are all the children of God by faith in Christ Jesus. 27For as many of you as have been baptized into Christ have put on Christ. 28There is neither Jew nor Greek, there is neither bond nor free, there is neither male nor female: for ye are all one in Christ Jesus. 29And if ye be Christ's, then are ye Abraham's seed, and heirs according to the promise.

Galatians 3:28 -There is neither Jew nor Greek, there is neither bond nor free, there is neither male nor female: for ye are all one in Christ Jesus.

'As you should know, the Gentile Nation was added to the Kingdom of God and given bringing forth the fruits thereof. And when the Gentiles were added to the kingdom, Peter stated surely God has no respect of person.'

According to Deuteronomy 28:68 there shell be a restoration of the whole house of Israel. 28:68-And the LORD shall bring thee into Egypt again with ships, by the way whereof I spake unto thee, Thou shalt see it no more again: and there ye shall be sold unto your enemies for bondmen and bondwomen, and no man shall buy you.

According to Act 7:6,And God spake on this wise, That his seed should sojourn in a strange land; and that they should bring them into bondage, and entreat them evil four hundred years.

According to "biblestudytools.com." 17.3.2.2. Valley of the Dry Bones as the source. The future restoration of the whole house of Israel is seen in Ezekiel's vision of the dry bones. God promises the spiritual regeneration of all of Israel (a condition of the New Covenant, Jer. Jer. 31:31) and the joining of both Northern and Southern Kingdoms under the future reign of David:

Then He said to me, "Son of man, these bones are the whole house of Israel. They indeed say, 'Our bones are dry, our hope is lost, and we ourselves are cut off!' As for you, son of man, take a stick for yourself and write on it: 'For Judah and for the children of Israel, his companions.' Then take another stick and write on it, 'For Joseph, the stick of Ephraim, and for all the house of Israel, his companions.' Then join them one to another for yourself into one stick, and they will become one in your hand. And when the children of your people speak to you, saying, 'Will you not show us what you mean by these?' - say to them, 'Thus says the Lord GOD: "Surely I will take the stick of Joseph, which is in the hand of Ephraim, and the tribes of Israel, his companions; and I will join them with it, with the stick of Judah, and make them one stick, and they will be one in My hand."' And the sticks on which you write will be in your hand before their eyes. Then say to them, 'Thus says the Lord GOD: "Surely I will take the children of Israel from among the nations, wherever they have gone, and will gather them from every side and bring them into their own land; and I will make them one nation in the land, on the mountains of Israel; and one king shall be king over them all; they shall no longer be two nations, nor shall they ever be divided into two kingdoms again.

They shall not defile themselves anymore with their idols, nor with their detestable things, nor with any of their transgressions; but I will deliver them from all their dwelling places in which they have sinned, and will cleanse them. Then they shall be My people, and I will be their God. David My servant shall be king over them, and they shall have one shepherd; they shall also walk in My judgments and observe My statutes, and do them. Then they shall dwell in the land that I have given to Jacob My servant, where your fathers dwelt; and they shall dwell there, they, their children, and their children's children, forever; and My servant David shall be their prince forever.

Moreover I will make a covenant of peace with them, and it shall be an everlasting covenant with them; I will establish them and multiply them, and I will set My sanctuary in their midst forevermore. My tabernacle also shall be with them; indeed I will be their God, and they shall be My people. The nations also will know that I, the LORD, sanctify Israel, when My sanctuary is in their midst forevermore." ' " (Eze. Eze. 37:11, Eze. 37:16-28)

In verses 15-28 Ezekiel mentions two sticks. I will not go into any detail here other than to say that they typify the northern (Israel) and southern (Judah) kingdoms which will again become one nation. This means, my friend, that there must not be any "ten lost tribes of Israel" at least, if there are, God knows where they are, and I am confident that it is not Great Britain which will be joined to them in that land!

Never the less, according to my research of scripture in the Hebrew original language, I find that God sent the Advocate to the people of Israel. He said don't call me master (rabbi) call me Teacher (Rabboni). The Spirit of Truth was in the Teacher. The Teacher Advocate of Truth TAUGHT what a man must do to live again and how a man's soul would return to God and enter the heavenly kingdom. THE YAOHUDIM WHO WERE FOLLOWERS OF THE HEBREW TEACHER AAY AH / ISH EE WAH, who did NOT bow to their IDOLS. The circumcised sanctified name of the Nazarene was given the Hebrew name in the Temple was YASHIYA and pronounced EE A SHO! and the head God YAH.

And one day, I Willie Stanfield dreamed a dream of a hidden doctrine. I walked through a room in house, where I was raised. The house was in re-decorating with three rooms and the rooms was all strewn in lavender slick curtains and very beautiful cloth furniture. I walked into the third room of my bedroom. No furniture was to be seen. Then behold! There were three closets in the room.

The first closet appeared and then was covered as if it never existed or faded away. It was just a wall where I knew the closet used to be at one time. It was the original closet. Then another closet appeared before me to the right side. I asked myself why the closet was changed. For the dresser that sat within was new. And behold! Another closet appeared to the left in the room. And I looked upon it and said, this is unnecessary, for it was a great change that the dresser was in the closet with the close-hanging rack above. There was no place to hang my close for it was completed. And in my dream, it was finished!

Dr. Yu said, "Now tell me, Mr. Stanfield, if any, what are your greatest fears in life?"

I know that to fear the Lord is the beginning of knowledge. I once thought I was only afraid of being afraid, but now I fear that someday I will see my demise in my own dream. Nevertheless, each day I awake and I rise in spite of my fears. There's an old saying, "Behind every cloud is a silver lining." Well, I guess I would rather die in my sleep than to die in the streets. There is a fine line between fear and respect. I think the two are interchangeable, and the only thing that separates the two is the end result of each.

One dream was the second time I saw my life flash before me. A friend and I were walking and all I could see was flashing lights. Everything was in slow motion. We walked toward the intersection. Traffic was very heavy. We stood by the road and watched for traffic to clear. We saw a young lady walking down the road. While we waited for the traffic to ease up, the young lady walked closer. I looked to see if the traffic was clearing. But still we could not cross. She began to get closer, then brushed up against my friend and walked past him.

Lights began to flash very quickly showing a sign of warning. It was a way of showing danger. Immediately I grabbed him by the shirt. I pulled him as we flew into the air. We escaped. The last thing I heard was,

"Oh my God, it almost hit me."

Then I awakened from this dream.

The next day in reality, I saw my dream reviled, when I ran into a friend. I met this friend through another friend, with whom I was more acquainted. His was a manager at Church's Fried Chicken in the neighborhood. I sometimes hung out and played Spades with them. Most of my time was spent them in the nightlife. We spent most of the time at the neighborhood club shooting pool. I connected with them in the daytime after work or on weekends.

On this day we decided to go to the gym to play basketball. We walked to the busy highway where the traffic was heavy. We walked to the middle of the turn lane. As we looked back behind us, we saw a lady walking along.

She was very attractive and caught the attention of every man who passed her. Car horns were blowing from both directions. We stood in the middle of traffic, but could not cross. It was dangerous to be in the middle of the road. I looked at the traffic about a half-mile from us. I observed a truck that was moving over slowly into the center turning lane. This truck was approaching us as the driver watched the young lady. My friend had no notion of the truck. It was headed toward us, but I didn't say anything. I thought the guy in the truck would focus back on the road. I tried to quickly cross. The highway traffic did not give us a break on either side.

My friend was looking at the female behind us. I reached out to my friend and pulled him back as I said, "Watch out for that truck." The driver didn't look up until he heard the noise from his side view mirror hitting my friend on the hand. When I pulled him back, he said,

"Oh my God! It almost hit me."

I then took a deep breath, and I realized we had escaped present danger. We had just survived a close call to death.

"Speaking of surviving a close call, as I sit here, Dr. Yu, and tell you my dream, I can't help but feel a bit uncomfortable. The lights are now out because of this Hurricane Katrina, and today is August 26, my birthday. I am stuck here in Miami on an important day of my life and this is the second time I have had to survive storms in the past two months. Just last month a small storm came through Jacksonville on the day I was changing jobs and making a career move."

On this day of the storm in Jacksonville, there was a large storm and the mall where I was working flooded. The strong waters came crashing down into the glass roof of the mall's walk-through area. I heard the voices of people screaming. People were trapped on the inside of the stores and could not go to their cars, and the drains could not keep up with the flow of water. Cars were stalling everywhere on the outside as people viewed this phenomenal act of Nature. They were at odds and every one spoke the same words: "I have never seen anything like this."

Water was up to the knees of people and in most places in the parking lots the water stood above the cars' and trucks' parking lights. The rain fell and thunder and lightning lasted for several hours at a rate I had never seen—and I have seen more than my share of storms. All of a sudden the rain completely stopped after two hours of massive flooding. I began to have visions of Bible scripture of the tremendous flood of Noah and the Ark. I can't imagine forty days and forty nights when two hours was to much for me.

At the end of the day, at the employee exit near the back of the dock, the water was so high we thought we would have to let employees leave from another exit. Within a half-hour of closing, the water was completely gone. I could not help but say,

"God works in mysterious ways."

It is quite ironic that although everyone knew the water was very high at the back door, the first associate to exit the door asked me,

"Will, did you pray for the water to leave?"

"Yes, I did," I said.

I opened the door for her, and said,

"You see God doesn't only move the mountain. He moves the water around the mountain also."

I have survived several close escapes, and I can't help but wonder,

"Is someone watching over me?"

All of a sudden, Dr. Yu's cell phone rang.

"Excuse me, Mr. Stanfield," he said. This is an important call I was expecting today."

Dr. Yu's phone call grew long. I became very relaxed and fell asleep and dreamed a dream. I had a vision of a great war, the likes of which had never been seen before. This war has been predicted from biblical times. It was as if the lion and the bear came face to face to be the king of the jungle. These kings knew of the destructive weapons and atomic bombs each nation was facing.

Then it came to pass: the great threat of pushing the button happened. Great armies from several nations were preparing for battle. All of a sudden, the sky unfolded as the clouds opened. It was as if the world were being crushed from a falling meteorite. The impact was so powerful. It shocked the earth off its axis.

In a wink of an eye everything came to a halt. It came to pass, after the smoke cleared, that the meteorite was actually a Solar Satellite Laser. The Lion of one nation intercepted the atomic bomb and destroyed it before launch. It shook the earth and this nation sustained massive destruction.

The people could not bury their love ones, for there was only smoke and bones as far as the eye could see. Ships came from afar with people covered from head to toe as they exited the ships and examined the scene.

I awakened as Dr. Yu finished his phone call. Once again he did not turn around as he began to write on his note pad. He wrote the word "escape" in large letters. His pad now had three words emblazoned on it:

Talent
Necessity
Escape

God continues to work with man in many
ways as he did in biblical days.

Psalm 124:7

Our soul is escaped as a bird out of the snare of the fowlers:
the snare is broken, and we are escaped.

Psalm 124:8

Our help is in the name of the LORD, who made heaven
and earth.

CHAPTER 4

My next dream that I will tell you is one of two dreams in which I foresaw a family member pass on. In reality, this love one who raised me from a boy was a man I respected greatly, a man who was there for me anytime I needed him and a man who was there to fight battles for me if needed.

I will not say he was a perfect man. He was a hard-working man with a courageous heart that supported the needs of the family.

Nevertheless we were not an untested family and I say today in this world, that a family that has not experienced some forms of imperfection is an untried and untested family. We all have imperfections. This love one did not hold any punches, when it came to correction. I was not a child to do harm– just a bit mischievous from time to time.

He would chastise me at home for disobedience in the classroom when my teacher would call. One period in my life I continued to misbehave in the classroom. I was in the fifth grade.

At this time I said something that was unspeakable as I spoke to my teacher. I would never speak those words again even as an adult. My teacher gave me a verbal warning for talking.

"If I hear you speak out of turn again, I will make a home visit to see your parents"

"It won't be today because my parent are working"

"I will go and visit your parents today"

Racial tension was highly present in these days. I was beginning to feel the impact at this tender age. On this day as I walked to school, a car of four men passed by, and one of the men spat on me. I remember picking up a brick to throw and hit the car, and had to run to school.

One of the most embarrassing whippings I ever received was in front of the fifth-grade classroom. One of my parents told me that he was going to come to my classroom and chastise me in front of the class. Well, this wasn't just a standard correction; this was a straight-up behind whipping. I will never forget that day when he told me to expect him at the end of the day. It was the longest day I ever had in school—waiting for my execution.

I told my friends that I was going to get corrected right in front of the classroom. I stared out the window all day thinking about whether or not I should run. I never ran before because I knew the family rule: he who runs would have a greater punishment on his head—or on his backside—in the end. At one point, I thought maybe he would never show up. Then all my friends saw him walk to the door and their heads turned my way as they looked at me with their eyes and mouths wide open.

He told my teacher he was here to teach me a lesson and then he called me up in front of the class. He gave me a good, old-fashioned spanking. I was glad when it was over. The punishment of waiting all day was worse than the whipping itself. To my surprise the whole classroom was mad at my teacher, but there was one little girl who thought the whole thing was hilarious. I took the butt whipping like a man because I couldn't cry in front of the class.

As I attempt to tell you more about this man who I admired, I am temped not to tell parts of this story because it would break a household rule. I was trained that household events of such matters should stay in the house. I believe in this rule and if it were not for the fact that I have a point, I would not speak of these events.

"However, I know that what is on record is between us, am I right Dr. Yu?"

Once assured, I continued.

In the house hold I was raised, it was instilled good values within the family, and I thank God they established a foundation of Christianity in our lives. There were times when I found serenity and security only in the Church or around Christian families. From the time to time, when I felt my spirit trapped or in trouble, I found peace only with a spiritual family or in the house of God. I can remember as far back as the age of ten, I would meet with other on Tuesdays at an elderly lady's home in the neighborhood. She would teach us the books of the Old and New Testament.

One night I felt a need to find safety. My young spirit led me to my Bible study teacher's home, where I found a safe haven of peace for the night. I was feeling strange and the thoughts running in my head gave me deep stomach emotions. I was most likely the only one awake that night in the house.

On this night, I stayed up and could not go to sleep. I heard the front door opening early in the morning. One parent was a no-nonsense person and had a fiery temper.

It became silent for a moment so I went back to my room and sat on the bed and held my face in my hands. I did not think things would get out of hand, but then I heard her screaming. I ran to the room and there I saw her over him, as he was face down on the floor. She had a knife to his back. I stood behind her and said,

"No, don't do it."

He said, "Don't let him see you do this."

She commanded me to go to my room.

I walked backwards a few feet as she stood up. Then I turned and went to my room. He would not hit her, as I saw him try to go into another room to avoid the fight. But she would never give up. She continued to provoke him. The argument moved to my room as he tried to walk away.

I hated putting myself in this situation at times. I would get between them and they would normally stop the fight. This night things began to get out of hand. When he walked into my room to get away from her, she hit with something and ran for the door. He then chased her to the door and stopped her from going out. She was trapped in between the door. He would not let her out. Then I heard her say,

"Stop, you are hurting me."

"I am not trying to hurt you. Are you going to stop?"

"Let me out."

He let her go.

Then I heard her say, "I'll get you. Where's the knife?"

"I am tired of this. Where is my gun?" he said.

I looked at them and looked at the gun. I picked up the double barrel shotgun. It was as heavy as a log but I ran with it, out the back door into the back yard. I ditched the gun over the fence and ran on instinct—and kept running.

I thought that if I took the gun and disappeared, this might divert their attention to me and stop the fight. So I ran to a place I felt safe, to the garage of my Bible study teacher's home. I was on the floor down beside the car as I began to catch my breath. I began to think about this incident as I lay there. I had flashbacks and visions from the first time I saw the gun. In another incident I remember regarding this same gun,

I was curious. When I was seven or eight years old, I went into my parents' room while they were at work. My Aunt Mary would keep me during the days when my parents were working. On this day I walked into the closet and saw the gun standing upright in the corner. The gun was kept loaded, and unfortunately my curiosity got the best of me.

I did not pick it up. I just looked at it for a few seconds, not knowing if it was loaded or not. I pushed down on the trigger. The gun went off with a loud boom. The shot went straight into the ceiling and up into the roof of the house. I could have harmed a family member or myself and I thought about this as I was in the garage and fell asleep beside the car on the concrete. I was thankful to God that the gun did not go off by mistake and hurt my parents.

I slept on the garage floor until the break of dawn. The sunlight awakened me. I was still in my pajamas. I ran quietly to the side door and knocked on it. It took my Bible teacher some time to come to the door, for it was very early in the morning. She finally came to the door in her robe and when she saw the desperate look on my face, she quietly opened the door.

"Come in. What is wrong with you?"

"There was a fight and I was frighten."

"Oh, I am sorry. Are you all right?"

"Yes, but I stayed in your garage last night."

"Why didn't you knock on the door?"

"I don't know. I guess I was just scared."

"Let me call your parents. They must be worried about you. Are you hungry?"

"No. I'm okay."

Once my parents arrived at my teacher's home, I thought they would be very upset with me but they were happy to see me and to know that I was safe. They searched for me into the early morning. My parents and my teacher talked for a while and my purpose was served. It was to stop the fight, but most likely at the expense of a family embarrassment. That was the least of their worries—the embarrassment.

My parents found the gun where I had hidden it that morning. I was glad he found it before someone else did. Maybe God used me to divert a situation before it got too far out of hand. Someone could have been injured that night and experiences have shown me that people do not always think before they act. A situation such as this can get out of hand and before I know it my whole life can flash and change in the blink of an eye. It is good today that legislators have put into effect a gun safety law for gun control and the protection of families. Even though this law is not bullet-proof, if it can save one person's life, that individual may be the one who saves your own life.

A few years later, my parents separated. A separation between a man and a woman when families are involved is hurtful. At this point I guess it is just the nature of the beast but what hurts the most is the entire family fills the pain. It is quite ironic how life patterns tend to follow suit in many cases. I have been involved in a relationship or two in the past where other's were .

I can get past the female I am involved with. Even the faces of the females I can forget, but I never forgot the faces of the little one. I have never met little one who did not love me once they got to know me. This is the type of love my parents expressed towards me. In essence no law or man in this world is perfect, except the law of God. But the impression of one man's good heart can leave a permanent effect on another life forever.

There is another dream I want to tell you about—the first of the two dreams in which I foresaw my parent member as he pass on. In this dream, I was standing in the driveway of my home in Baton Rouge. I saw a construction machine in the form of a man. It was building a bridge with its hands. The machine was laying brick and spreading mortar at the same time as it structured the bridge. It was in a fast and orderly manner. This amazed me—to see a machine perform in a robot-type manner. All of the sudden, a block from the bridge hit me in the head as I was looking up. Then out of nowhere I saw myself talking to one parent over the phone. I was informed about the passing of another parent. His name was the only thing I understood. I saw another stone flying in my direction. I awakened from this dream.

The next day in reality after I awakened, I received a call from one of my parents. I was told that a love one had passed on. The day after we spoke, I began to create my first patented invention. It was based on a simple concept, which I have experimented with long before. I would take a small magnifying glass and a piece of paper. The heat rays from the sun burned straight through the paper. Turning the magnifying glass to a particular angle would create a concentrated heat ray and burn through the surface. Can you imagine this on a larger scale? It could be created in conjunction with a satellite laser. Using this concept on this enormous scale can create a laser beam. This mass-destructive design could be used in the United States Defense system. Now, I dedicate this new invention in the name of that parent. I will call it the "J. F. T. Solar Satellite Laser."

I described the dream to Dr. Yu and he began to give me a prognosis. He said, "I think this dream was a symbol of something near and dear to you. You have made an important discovery. Nevertheless, it will be for a contribution of mankind that can cause massive destruction."

After he spoke those words, he picked up his pen but it fell to the floor. I knew that he must turn around because the pen rolled to the floor behind him. But Dr. Yu simply rolled his chair back with his feet and picked up his pen.

He wrote on his note pad the word "machine" in large letters.

God continues to work with man in many
ways as he did in biblical days.

2 Chronicles 26:15

And he made in Jerusalem engines, invented by cunning men,
to be on the towers and upon the bulwarks, to shoot arrows
and great stones withal. And his name spread far abroad; for
he was marvelously helped, till he was strong.

CHAPTER 5

"Dr. Yu, before I talk to you about my next dream, I would like to tell you about the person involved and give some background on this person."

"She is a very interesting lady with some very peculiar gifts. She was a person whom I met when I was about nine or ten years old. I respected her highly and looked to her for guidance.

I really began to draw near and highly respect this Lady when an elderly relative had a stroke. Lady helped take care of me during these difficult times. She was like a guardian figure to me. We became very good friends and I felt strongly that I could trust her.

When I left Pensacola and moved to Jacksonville, Lady was the last person I said my farewell to. We stood on the outside of my house. We asked each other one question as we departed.

"Do you trust anybody?"

I looked very deeply into her eyes, as I paused and said,

"Yes. I can trust anyone to a limited extent, but I don't trust anybody totally."

"Well, I don't trust anyone," she said.

"Do you think I will be successful in Jacksonville?" I asked.

"You will make more money than you thought you would ever make in your life. But why are you still working that job?"

So I just looked at her with a puzzled look in my eyes. As I thought about the question, she asked me again if I trusted anyone. She caught me off-guard. I really did not understand where she was going with the question. Even before that question, my feelings were that I can trust anyone to a degree, but I don't put my trust in any man totally.

When she asked me the question of trust and said that she did not trust anyone, it was as if she was trying to make a point. She did not elaborate and I did not ask any further questions on the matter.

I understand now what she predicted years ago. I will tell you her stories. It may be that she did not want me to tell the stories she once told me. Maybe she thought people would portray her to be something other than a psychic and healer. I pray that this world has become further advanced and knows there is more to our mind than meets the eye.

I have to admit there is many things in the supernatural world I don't understand, but I won't let my vague insight put me in a state of being small-minded. If it were not for these stories being a part of my understanding that leads to my dream, I would not tell the stories.

Lady told me some very interesting stories in the past that really disturbed me, which leads to my next dream.

Her experiences were with people who asked her for help. She fought against spirits in high places. Even if you do not believe these stories, it does not mean they don't exist. I once heard of the story of a visit that Lady made to someone's home. She entered the house and stepped through the front door and immediately felt a cold chill through her whole body. She began to back out immediately.

"I can't go in there. Something is not right in this house. Something evil is in there and I cannot enter. Check around the front room," she told her friends.

They all began to check the room, and finally behind the couch found only a snake's head, but no body. Its tongue was twirling around, darting in and out of its mouth and its eyes were open.

I have heard that in order to destroy a snake, you must first destroy its head. But I have never heard of a snake's head surviving without its body. I think it would take some very serious evil to accomplish this. I must not underestimate the limitations of the devil's devices. When fighting against evil in a spiritual world, such things in high places that may seem impossible just may be possible.

It's quite easy not to believe the things that I have not seen or the things I fear. This is often the best way to deal with something feared or something that one is trying to avoid. I do believe this. Something I haven't seen can exist. What I don't know can hurt me. If it weren't for believing in things I haven't seen, faith would not exist.

Another story was a satanic story. This really grieved me how some people who this Lady tried to help were under witchcraft. To reach a level of evil that will make you hurt a family is unspeakable. It is an evil beyond measure.

This was a family of three where everyone was infected. This was not just an ordinary infection. Lady predicted the outcome of this targeted event. The family did not seek Lady's help in time. The family was given food by a person who sought to harm. The food was mixed with some type of evil substance. Once the family ate the food, they grew lizards and snakes in their stomachs.

This process took a long time to develop. Pain and torment were the result of suffering. Once the evil had fully developed, it then exited the body. I did not hear what happened to all but one member was found on the floor with a huge hole in her stomach. A king cobra was in a corner in an upright position when rescue personnel entered the home.

There are medical studies that contradict this theory. It would be impossible to grow something in the stomach area because of the digestive system with acids that break down what we eat. But working with evil sprits of this nature, as with God, who knows what may be possible?

There are methods of completing the process other than just the physical act. The chanting and burning of different herbs completes the process. Witchcraft is one of the oldest sins of biblical time. In one biblical story, God instructed the Israel to put all of their books of witchcraft into the fire or they would be destroyed. Last but not least, God would not have me ignorant of the devil's devices.

This last story is a ghost of an experience I often felt as an adult. It is a strange story but, strangely, not so uncommon. I know that other people have experienced this also. I know this because the expression of "The witch is riding your back" is a label given to this spirit-haunting feeling long before I experienced it. I was asleep and felt my eyes open. I was trying to move and could not. It is a very uncomfortable feeling to be trapped and have no control over my body in the bed. I began to realize after several of these dreams that if I could only move a finger I could awaken. At times this would work, but sometimes it would not. Once I realized the only thing that was really open was my mind, not my eyes. I would call the name, "Jesus," and I would completely awaken. Well, believe me, this was not just a dream. It was a spirit brand new, and the only way out was the way through.

I continued with this next dream, which was one of the strangest dreams of all. Dreaming of spirits is always uncomfortable. I would feel the spirits both in my dreams and on the outside of my body. In this particular dream, I was fighting off a spirit in the form of a snake. I was in my home in Pensacola. I ran upon a snake. I tangled with the snake in a long, exhaustive battle. No matter what I hit the snake with or how many times I cut the snake, I could not defeat it. I was tired and drained in my sleep.

Well, I have learned to master certain dreams when I cannot overcome a situation like this in my sleep. I learned to create a diversion by running into the air to escape from predators. This method would normally work at any time in my dreams. This time, my method did not work. The snake was able to fly with me.

All of a sudden, a strange thing appeared to me in my dream—Bananas! The peelings of the bananas were dried out. I threw the banana peels at the snake, and destroyed my predator with them. Then I awakened from this dream.

The few days in reality I saw the aftermath of my dream, as I followed my regular routine. I would stop by and say "Good morning" to the Lady as I passed by her home. She told me she was fighting a bad ghost or spirit that someone sent her. This spirit would stand outside in her yard, and she had a difficult time getting rid of it. In witchcraft, one way to send a ghost or evil spirit to someone is to move a tombstone in the direction of that person's home. Words are chanted and the ghost is released. The ghost then haunts and tries to torment this person. Lady told me that there were methods she used to stop this spirit.

Putting hard-boiled eggs in her front yard kept the spirits from entering her yard. Brushing animal's blood over the door kept the spirit from entering her home. She said this method normally would drive a spirit away, but this spirit was strong and she could not drive it away. It just stood on the outside in her yard.

I believe this is a method that was derived from a biblical act. God sent His Spirit to homes during Passover in order that the first-born inside the homes would be protected. Moses was instructed to tell the people of Israel to brush blood over their doorframes. That way, the spirit passed over.

I knew that she was a strong person in her profession of fighting against bad spirits. I felt that if this were something she could not defeat, I did not want to be around it.

I began to tell her about the dream I had the night before and I explained to her the great difficulty I had defeating the snake. I suggested she use banana peels, just as I had to defeat the spirit. Well, I spoke with her in the next few days. It was a surprise to me when she told me that the method I gave her from this dream was indeed successful.

I finished telling this dream to Dr. Yu. He said, "Your dream has shown you protection for yourself and others who are near you. Your dreams have revealed how you can conquer and have victory over your enemies." After he spoke those words, he picked up his pen and pad with his back towards me.

He wrote on his note pad the word "ghost" in large letters.

God continues to work with man in many
ways as he did in biblical days.

Jeremiah 23:28

The prophet that hath a dream, let him tell a dream; and he
that hath my word, let him speak my word faithfully. What
is the chaff to the wheat? saith the LORD.

Proverbs 16:2

All the ways of a man are clean in his own eyes; but the
LORD weigheth the spirits

Isaiah 8:19

And when they shall say unto you, Seek unto them that have
familiar spirits, and unto wizards that peep, and that mutter:
should not a people seek unto their God? for the living to
the dead?

CHAPTER 6

Dr. Yu said, "Now, Mr. Stanfield, tell me about the first time you remember falling in love, the last love you can remember and the outcomes."

I remember only two teachers from my elementary school days. It is quite strange because, as I said earlier, I remember only the face, of the teacher with whom I fell in love, and not her name. On the other hand, I remember the name, but not the face, of the teacher whom I disliked more than any. I was only in the fifth grade when I fell in love with my teacher. She was the most beautiful lady I had ever seen, and her intelligence matched her beauty.

I remember once asking my parent during the Christmas season if I could buy my teacher a gift. So she took me shopping, and I picked out a pair of earrings that were astonishingly beautiful. This was the first time I had purchased a gift for a female with whom I had fallen in love. In the old days they called it puppy love. I guess you wouldn't think a boy of my tender age would know anything about love. Today there is no puppy in me for I am still the some old hound I used to be, and hearts remain the same.

I can remember as if it were yesterday when I gave her the Christmas gift. She immediately smiled, took them out of the box, put them on and said, "Thank you." Well, I'm sure it wasn't her intention, but it really turned me on. When the summer was over and I returned to school, I went directly to her classroom to say "Hello." To my surprise, there was another teacher sitting in her chair.

I asked this teacher why she was sitting in the chair. She said, "This is my chair this year. Your former teacher will no longer be here."

You could not imagine the feelings and confusion in my mind at that young age. This was my first lost love. I felt I would never see her again. I heard of her many years later when I went to college at Southern University. I saw someone who know her, which was one of the barbers at the college barbershop to which I often made visits.

The last love I remember took part in my next dream.

Dr. Yu interrupted me to say,

"Before you tell me about this next dream, give me some history on the relationship."

Well, in the beginning of this relationship I remember walking three miles to visit her in the middle of a summer day. Reaching my destination, I waited in the park across the street from her house. I sat high atop the jungle-gym, so that she could see me from her front window. Waiting patiently I watched for the curtain in the window to be pulled as a sign that she was aware of my presence.

Only minutes had passed when I saw the sign and she walked out the door. Her beautiful hair hung below her shoulders, swaying back and forth as she gave off a controlling air. Her stride showed a self-confident, slight swagger like that of a fashion model. She took the short cut to the park and I met her at the park.

Because there was no gate for her to enter, I reached out my arms over the fence. As I grabbed her by the waist, I lost eye contact. I pulled her up. Her feet hit the center of the fence and her hand went to the top of the fence post. She then placed her hands on my shoulders and I held her by the waist. As her body weight increased, my fingers went deeper into her waist. She was then over the fence when I pulled her to me, and our eyes reconnected.

She put her hands on my chest. My heart began racing wildly. I did not know if it was from lifting her over the fence or from just the way she made me feel. When I slid my hands up from her waist to her face, her breathing turned harsh as she inhaled deeply. We maintained eye contact, but when I pulled her to me, she closed her eyes.

Breathing from my nose she held her breath until the end. When I gave up contact, she exhaled. She captivated me as I instinctively wrapped my arms around her and whispered in her ear softly, "I love you." She looked at me as if it were the first time I had spoken these words to her. She would not turn away as she gazed at me intensely. It was a sweet-tasting savor on my tongue, giving me thoughts of strawberries.

It was now the last days before my final departure. I made plans to move to Pensacola and I shortly received an offer from a construction company to work in the field of architectural drafting. This company had just moved into the area and signed me on commission.

I looked forward to returning to the city I grew up in. But I had to leave my love behind, and I did not look forward to that. Before I departed, for the second time in our relationship, I visited her home. During my first visit I met her guardian, but this time no one was nowhere to be found and we were alone.

She was aware of my immediate departure to Florida and of my opportunity for a new job offer. At this time I had known her for at least one year and we both were sad knowing the choices. We both spoke about a relationship but the long distance had more disadvantages than possibilities. We made promises to one another and we both thought that our love had no boundaries and that distance would not keep our souls apart.

Then we both took a chance knowing the circumstances at the time. We were afraid that we would not see each other for a long time. In addition, I was hoping no one would follow their usual pattern and not come home at this time. I don't know if her fear was because she did not know if someone would show up or because this was her first time, for she was a virgin.

I wanted to be gentle and show compassion, for when she wept I asked, Do you want to stop?

She replied, 'No' and then I consummated our bond. She made me feel alive.

The next day was the last day I would see Baton Rouge for a long time, so I visited a good friend in the neighborhood whose name was Frank. I had known him from the days of elementary school and on throughout high school. It seems as if everywhere I showed up, he was there too. He even showed up in special programs such as Upward Bound and at the same college I attended.

Frank and I had a long talk and reminisced about the past. The last thing we talked about was my plans to marry this particular female, with whom he was well acquainted.

Not often did I see Frank in a serious state of mind, but this was one time I saw another side to him. He gave some advice I remember to this day.

He said, "You should think about this marriage.

I don't think you know her like you should. This is a big step and there is something about her you might need to consider first."

It was not that he had a relationship with her in the past, but he knew a friend who knew of some serious emotional issues and recurring events. He also questioned her relationship ethics.

I told him, "I know you are looking out for my best interest, and I appreciate this because you are my friend. But, how well do we know anyone in this type of relationship? You can be with someone, it seems, forever and not really know them. If it were not for taking chances, I think we would lose more in life than we would gain. You know the old saying, 'It is better to have loved and lost than to have never loved at all."

"Well you are my boy and if this is what you really want, I am happy for you and I wish you well.

I departed to the East Coast. The last I heard of Frank, he had gone to East Coast and was living in New York. In Pensacola, I tried to keep up the intensity of my long-distance relationship with my lady friend, as we were trying to reach for higher ground.

Finally, we found common ground and decided that she would move to Pensacola and we would be married. The next day, a relative and I departed from Pensacola to Baton Rouge, driving overnight. We checked into a hotel, stayed one night, and picked her up from her home the next day. Then, we drove back to Pensacola.

We arrived after traveling straight through an early morning drive, and we were both happy now that we had reached the beginning of that higher ground. Because we were staying at a relative's home we had separate rooms. I stayed in my own, and she slept in the other room until we were married.

We were married in the courthouse and everything seemed to be a bed of roses. She was in school and I was working for a construction company as a draftsman. The company would bid on a number of construction bids but with a ruthless operation of underhanded overbidding the company did not develop well.

Then everything went from bad to worse. It left a very spooky feeling when I came upon her in a trancelike state. I would find her just sitting with her eyes open, not saying a word. It was as if her body was there, but her mind was in another world. I would have to sometimes shake her to wake her up.

We finally consulted with Lady to try and make more sense of this because at this point, I knew this was not natural. The Lady I knew gave some very interesting observations about her problem. Lady's spiritual view and advice was this:

She received $50,000 from a life insurance policy. An evil woman, who practiced voodoo, had her own motive of obtaining the insurance money. This woman had a lot of influence and if she could eliminate her somehow, this would bring the money closer to her because the money would go to the next of kin—who she was associated with. Well, she finally received the help she needed from Lady after a long drawn-out battle, and I began to see her come back to reality.

Just when I thought everything was on track, it turned out to be the calm before the storm. Then the things my friend Frank warned me about began to happen. One thing he did mention was that she was an attention seeker. The signs were there. One day, she came home after school with a male classmate to study for a test. Well, I am very observant and have pretty good judgment about body language. I could see behind his eyes when I looked at him. I watched his body language as I walked away from him, I knew his intentions, and I was sure she knew his intentions also.

After she introduced me, I walked calmly out the door and I knew what my next move would be. I intended to wait until they became very relaxed at the table and walked back in brand new, if you know what I mean. If this were a study group it would not have been such a big thing. It is not always what you do, but sometimes how you do it that keeps your head above water. Well, to invite this type of action into my house was a setup I don't think either of them was ready for.

My next step was to go two doors down and sit on another porch, not let off steam but to build up tension. The Lady came out of the house and asked why I was sitting on the porch.

"Oh . . . I am just waiting."

"I don't like the sound of that. Come inside. Let me talk to you. What is your problem?"

"There is no problem yet. There will be in a minute when I go down to the house and run everything with a heart beat out of there."

When I told her what the problem was, she closed the door, locked it, stood in front of it and would not let me out. She picked up the phone and called her.

"What are you doing?" she asked.

"Are you out of your mind? You better get that boy out of there before this man comes back. I can't hold him for long."

I crept out the back door of the house because I knew that she was giving her time to get the man out. By the time I got back to the house, only two doors down, he was gone. This was a good thing because my thoughts were rough. Not that it was so much his fault being there, but I was going to give him one opportunity to get out and one wrong word from him would have set me off.

There was a huge argument. This put a big strain on our relationship. The last words I remember saying are,

"Who do you think you are?

It all went from bad to worse when the next day, I went to work and the bid that the company made fell through. The client loved my work drawings, but the contractor I was working for overpriced the bid. It was obvious what they were trying to do. Another company came in and received the contract with a fair bid.

Unfortunately, the day was not over. When I returned, she was not there. It was getting late and I received a call from my manager, stated she was in a car accident.

"Hello?"

"Hey, Stanfield. This is Bob."

"Yes?"

"Look, there's a problem."

"What?"

"She's ok. She was in a car accident and she said the two of you had a fight yesterday. She said you were angry with her and if she called, she didn't think you would come. So she called me."

"I'm on my way."

This just showed me another way that she was handling personal business the wrong way. I did not want my home mixed with my business of work. Why did she not call someone in the family who already knew about the fight? Nevertheless, I am not a shallow person. I would respond to an incident of such a serious nature that requires my attention regardless of a family fight. I went and I supported her.

Not long after this, I began to get tired of her suspicious behavior and I was not happy with my job or with how things were going. The honeymoon was over.

Well, as I have heard, some things never change in the hearts of others. We hit that bump in the road, that place which comes in every relationship. It's where two people have to look around and decide whether to go forward or whether to pull back, that place where things stop being perfect and start being more real.

We decided to pull back and separate. She went back to Baton Rouge and I stayed in Pensacola. Even so, we stayed in contact and she traveled that long distance to visit me from time to time. Well, after a few months she persuaded me to move back to Baton Rouge with her. Everything was good for a few months—until I saw another sign when we took an afternoon walk around the apartment complex. We walked to the swimming pool area and stood just outside the fence. A male schoolmate recognized me but we did not know one another well. We just played ball on the basketball court in our school days. He spoke to me from the other side of the pool.

"Hey, man. What's up? You went to Istrouma High School, didn't you?"

"Yes, I remember you."

"How are you?"

"I am great, and you?"

"Hey! This is my…..," I said.

"I'm sorry. I thought she was your relative ."

I could see that he was sincere about his actions and I could see his point because I thought she was overly responsive to him. Plus, this was not the first time someone assumed we were siblings.

On one occasion when we were in the neighborhood store just a week before, we were mistaken to be relatives by the counter cashier as she complimented my eyes and flirted with me aggressively in front of her. I quickly responded, "This is the apple of my eye"

"Oh, I'm sorry I thought she was a relative."

"That's okay. Others have made that mistake as well."

I could understand how people might think we were siblings, so there was no sense in getting angry if the incident was handled appropriately. Nevertheless, I was upset with her once we returned home because she had acted inappropriately in front of my schoolmate.

I was willing to accept that this would happen from time to time. However, the relationship once again began to turn in the wrong direction. So I decided to go back to Pensacola. She drove when I was moving back to Pensacola and a new found relative of her rode with her.

I assumed it was a relative since she introduced him as such and this was the first time I had ever seen him. However, at this point I didn't trust her at all. Besides, I just really needed to get away from her before I got into some serious trouble that I might regret because of her infidelity. Her ways were driving me crazy. I was back in Pensacola for approximately three months and we talked often over the phone. Once, I had a very uncomfortable and spooky dream about her the night before we talked.

In this dream, I arrived at an apartment building and looked up at a window. I saw the woman in my relationship trying to speak to me. She pointed down to the ground. I looked down to see a letter written in red ink. I picked up the letter and tried to read it. It was a full-page letter but I could not understand what was written. I tried several times and felt a sense of present danger. I walked up the staircase to the front door. An old lady on the inside said to me,

"Please don't go up there. You won't like what you'll see."

I walked up the stairs where there was fog that came up to my knees. I entered the building and walked through a hallway. It was a very spooky feeling. There were many doors on each side, all the way down the hall. Every door was open. I walked through the hallway and looked from side to side. In each room, were people were lying in a bed. On every bed was a couple. Some rooms even had more than one couple. Each person was naked and appeared to have their eyes closed. As I arrived at the end of the hallway, the strangest thing happened. A mop with a bucket was in the corner and it appeared to have muddy water in it. The bucket turned over and out of nowhere appeared an old lady. Then she tried to clean it up, and I awakened from the dream.

It is quite coincidental in reality I saw this dream appear with open eyes, the very next day she was out of town in Baton Rouge. She called me and asked me to come visit her. The very next day, I got on a Greyhound bus and left for Baton Rouge from Pensacola. When we met, I grabbed her hand, and greeted her.

Shortly we arrived at her apartment complex. I remember the strange feeling I had as I stepped out of the car. It was a déjà vu feeling, as if I had been here before. When we walked into the house, I went upstairs. I took a hot bath and went into the bedroom. I laid her on the bed in the heat of passion. We began to make love, but all of a sudden, she said,

"Stop! I became frustrated. It turned me off so I just turned over and chilled.

"Would you like for me to go out and get something for us to eat?" she asked.

"If you're hungry," I replied.

"Okay, I'll be right back."

I waited on the bed. The strangest feeling came over me. All of a sudden I turned over and, for no apparent reason, I opened the bottom dresser drawer. I reached down and pulled out the first thing that was on top.

I was very angry with this letter and knew she would continue to hide this matter from me. Approximately twenty minutes later, she returned from the store. When she came inside the house, I was upstairs angrily waiting and pacing the floor. I needed to clear my head quickly because I did not want to do something I might regret. When she walked up the stairs to the bedroom, I said,

"Take me back to the bus station."

With a panicked look, she said,

"What is wrong?"

"Just take me back to the bus station or I will call a taxi."

She continued to ask me what was wrong, but I tried once again to avoid the issue. I was too angry to talk about it but she pushed the issue persistently. I wanted to just grab her by her neck, but I decided that she wasn't worth it. I pulled the letter out and demanded she explain. She said,

"This is MY letter!" as she grabbed it, tore it up and then flushed it down the toilet.

When I returned to Pensacola, several messages from her were there. Finally, when I did speak to her, she wanted to give me an explanation of the letter—and what an explanation it was. Just when I thought I had heard it all. Just imagine this:

The next day, her aunt called me from New Orleans, to plead her case. She said,

"Give her a second chance. She is confused."

The next words she said were words that cut like a two-edged sword. (I am just paraphrasing her words.) I will let you imagine what she said.

Then she said,

"She's getting brainwashed. You need to give her a chance to make this right."

I said, "The first wrong was to cheat. The second wrong was to hide it, and two wrongs cannot make this right."

"Dr. Yu, what do you think about this dream?"

He said, the dream is giving you an open view from the inside of the window where she stood to the outside of reality where you stand. The naked couples on the bed, which appeared to have their eyes closed, represented the end of the relationship between a man and woman. The mopping up of muddy water by the elderly woman indicates that something about this situation was unclean. Her aunt was the old lady in the dream who was only trying to clean up this situation. The dream showed you the deceptions of the woman in an adulterous relationship. All of a sudden, one of the stuffed animals, a bobcat, ran across the floor to the door, then ran back to the corner and said,

"Today's dreams may be tomorrow's reality."

"Did you here that, Dr. Yu?"

"No, what did you hear?"

"The bobcat ran across the floor and then spoke to me."

"It's not possible. The animals are stuffed," he replied. Maybe you are suffering from a little postpartum depression and you are seeing things."

I glanced at Dr. Yu with his back still towards me. After he spoke those words, he picked up his pen and pad.

He wrote on his note pad the word "deception" in large letters.

God continues to work with man in many
ways as he did in biblical days.

Job 42:10

And the LORD turned the captivity of Job, when he prayed
for his friends: also the LORD gave Job twice as much as he
had before.

Job 42:11

Then came there unto him all his brethren, and all his
sisters, and all they that had been of his acquaintance
before, and did eat bread with him in his house: and they
bemoaned him, and comforted him over all the evil that the
LORD had brought upon him: every man also gave him a
piece of money, and every one an earring of gold.

CHAPTER 7

The next dream was very difficult for me to digest. This involved the second person in my life that passed on. I loved this person more than anyone in this world. She was a lady with a heart of gold whom I deeply respected. A love and bond was created from the day I was born and we grew to be inseparable. The only love I saw her show greater or equal to her love for me was her love for God.

I will always remember the story she told me of her closes relative when she passed on. I was between one and two years old. The way she talked about the times her love one spent with me made me think there was a greater love than ever that existed and I was too young to remember. I don't remember her and the only remembrance that I will ever have of her will be the story about when she was buried, that was told to me.

She held me throughout the funeral even at the burial ground. She told me that holding me close to her at the burial ground kept her at peace. It is said that when a loved one passes on in the Lord there is no sorrow, for they are at peace in the Lord. The relative who held me at the say event, she was calm up until she heard me for the first time speak these words. I spoke my first words-"She sleep" in a sentence as they lowered her in the ground.

She looked into my eyes as reality hit her. She could not hold her peace any longer, as she began to call out to the grave. She suffered several strokes from the time I was 10 to 17 years old, recovering very well each time. She recovered her speech and learned how to walk again. She was a strong woman.

Some of my most exciting moments were spent living in Pensacola when school was out. I spent the summer with this relative. She was a hard worker in the church and attended services at least three times a week.

My friends in the church were like family. We spent plenty of time in the church and had some good times when we visited one another in our homes. I really enjoyed the Goldsmith and Pryor families where I spent most of my time. There were many church activities that kept us out of the street. I enjoyed playing in the summer basketball leagues and going on trips to other congregations. When I became a teenager, I began to spend my summers in Baton Rouge in the Upward Bound Program.

My summers were now spent on the campus of Southern University of Baton Rouge. It was not until I received my degree from college that I returned to Pensacola. After college, I moved to Pensacola and finally returned to the church where I was baptized. I became very committed to working in the church where it seemed like old times. Even though the church had moved to a much larger and more elaborate building, I could not help but miss the little building where we grew up.

Nevertheless, one of my most memorable moments in this church took place with a mirror painting I drew and painted over the pool pit wall. It was so strange to me because I had never painted a picture of such great size. This painting was approximately nine-by-fourteen feet and covered the whole wall. It had been six or seven years since I had painted a picture. Well, to pick up a brush and attempt to pull off this job was almost like a foreign language to me. I gathered my equipment, assembled everything and sat in a chair in the pool pit to think. I remember the minister asked as he looked at the wall, "Have you ever drawn a painting this big?"

"No"

"Do you think you can handle a big job of this nature?"

"If I don't think I can, then I am already defeated."

"Well, I will leave it to you."

Then the minister went to his office as I stood there to think what approach I should take. My first approach was to pray for guidance. I decided to paint a baptismal scene. It took me a week to finish such a large picture and we kept the curtain closed until the painting was complete the next Sunday. To my surprise this was the best drawing and painting I had ever displayed.

At the time of unveiling, the minister who baptized me delivered a sermon on prayer. There were many scriptures this day on prayer and he spoke of giving thanks to God and of praying without ceasing in all things. He gave an example in the closing of his sermon.

"I once saw a young man that I watched from a distance on his knees in prayer. For several days I saw this young man in prayer before he started his task. Several days I walked from my office when I knew he was in the building and I saw him in prayer. I prayed with him when he didn't know I was there. I also saw his faith as he rose and looked at the painting and sat in this chair. For I say to the Church, Pray without ceasing for God is always there. For where there are two or more gathered together in His name there He is in their midst. Now will you bow your heads with me in prayer?"

As he began to pray, I reflected on a vision that came to me after prayer when I was sitting at a desk in my room as I drew my very first drawing. As I sat in the church and viewed my picture from afar, I was sure this was a talent given to me by God.

As time passed, I fell away from my talent. I began to realize if I didn't use it, I could lose it. For God will give, and He will take away. Work was very slow in the small town with mostly military and light industry being the only good employment. Because of the difficulty finding good employment in Pensacola, after a while I became idle. As it is written in the scriptures, "An idle mind is the devil's workshop." Well, a devil's workshop is what I found.

On one early night on the way to the store, I stopped to play a game of pool at the pool hall. The tables were full and the place was filled with cigarette smoke so I went outside to avoid the heavy smoke and waited on a table. I had a clear view of the table until it was my turn to play with my fifty cents. Two men were talking and one of the men and I exchanged unkind words. As he approached me with his friend, I began to see the odds were uneven, so I evened the battleground when I pulled out a gun. They stepped back, turned around and headed back into the pool hall.

I then proceeded to leave the area. As I walked several blocks, trying to cross the street, the sheriff's department was called. The traffic was so heavy I could not cross the street or go to the center of the road. I was only two blocks from my home and I felt trapped. All of a sudden, out of nowhere, law enforcement stopped me. The night was not over yet, for I was very angry. I felt that I was defending myself by running off the two men with my gun. I was not charged with carrying a concealed firearm. I was charged with attempted robbery! Little did I know that the man I had the conflict with was related to the store manger and they tried to set me up with a robbery charge.

I was distressed and disturbed by this and at this point anything that entered my comfort zone this night of my detainment would definitely alarm me. So I tried to stay to myself, but I guess I was in the wrong place to have a comfort zone. I was sitting in a cell waiting for processing with only one other person in the holding cell with me.

I said to the warden,

"Hey, could I get my one phone call?"

He ignored me, so I said a little louder.

"Excuse me, sir, when can I make a phone call?"

"Hey man, won't you shut up?" The guy in the holding cell said.

I was in no mood to be messed with. I snapped at him.

"Who's talking to you, punk?" In a menacing voice I added, "I hope they put us in the same cell when we get back there. I'll see how much you got to say then."

Well, the look on his face was as if he just put his foot in his mouth. He looked down as if he really didn't want to go into the next cell with me that night. The front desk overheard our conversation. I believe that is why we did not end up in the same cell.

We finished the first part of processing and we were separated. I went to another holding cell with about ten other men. I felt at peace for a while because everyone was quiet and seemed to mind his own business. I sat on a bench, established a comfort zone and, as the old saying goes,

"When in Rome, do as the Romans do."

About twenty minutes later another person was put in the cell and just when I thought everything was at ease in this environment, it turned out to be only an illusion. It was a dark rain before a hurricane. Soon it became like an ancient Coliseum event, crowded with spectators facing battle. Another male walked in and paced around the cell for about ten minutes running his mouth about nothing as if his directives were to everyone in the cell. Everyone ignored him and gave him freedom of speech as long as he stayed his distance. Then he began to get a little too close for comfort, walking past everyone as we sat on the bench. He stopped in front of me, continuing to rant and rage. He was definitely too close for comfort.

He looked directly at me and said,

"These punks make me sick."

I stood up from the bench.

"Say what?" I said. "You don't know me. You need to check your vision. You don't see no punk in me."

He began to slowly back up to the other side of the room near the cell bars as he continued to talk. I was fine with that as long as he did not challenge me. But one of the other men shouted out.

"Hey, they are tripping in here. Let me out of here."

We were put in separate holding cells by ourselves. I slept for about two hours and then another person was put in the cell with me. Everything was fine until the food trays came to the cell. The trays was left at the bars and the other man ran to the cell and grabbed both trays.

I was quick to defend myself, for I was still in no mood to be messed with.

"Where do you think you are? This ain't Burger King. You won't just have it your way today. Give up one of the trays."

I had no problem getting my tray. He said nothing and just gave me the tray. It was now time for blood work and after that, final processing. I was able to get my first phone call when they put me in a cell that had phones. Then I was led down a long hall to my permanent cell. As I took this walk there were many large cells of men that each averaged approximately twenty to thirty people. Each cell seemed to have different forms of activities. Some were playing card games; others were just sitting and joking around. When I arrived at my house cell I saw some people walking around. Some were walking in a fast pace to exercise. I went upstairs to my bunk where there were four beds per room.

I stayed in the room and slept for only a minute because one of the men came into the room and I quickly sat up to see why. He said nothing as he looked at me and handed me a small Bible. It had a bookmark in it. I opened it and read II Corinthians 12:7-10. I will never forget that chapter for it read:

And lest I should be exalted above measure though the abundance of the revelations, there was given to me a thorn in my flesh, the messenger of Satan to buffet me, lest I be exalted above measure / For this thing I be sought the Lord thrice, that it might depart from me / And he said unto me, "My grace is sufficient for thee, for my strength is made perfect in weakness." Most gladly therefore will I rather glory in my infirmities, that the power of Christ may rest upon me / Therefore I take pleasure in infirmities, in reproaches, in necessities, in persecution, in distresses for Christ's sake, for when I am weak I am strong.

I have always heard that God works in mysterious ways and I was experiencing firsthand God's power even in the midst of my deepest dismay. I felt that God has always tried to use me in a special way. How, I don't know, even to this day. His mysteries are deep and that's all I can say, for I am like a shovel digging to find my way.

It was funny in one sense. The man wanted to show his experience in being a repeat offender by trying to give me advice in order to lighten my so-called sentence. The next day was my court day or "rabbit court," as they called it. Surprisingly everything went well and I was released on my own recognizance and given a public defender and a future court date. I was not optimistic about having a public defender on my side and I was thinking about hiring a private lawyer.

After meeting with the public defender I felt more inclined to think my most favorable chance would be to give her the opportunity to clear me of the robbery charges. She also assured me that she would send out investigators and research my case. I really thought she went beyond the call of duty in order to clear my name before my court date. After all was said and done, I was in fact cleared of the chargers. My gun was returned to me because I had a concealed firearms license. However, I did get rid of it because I realized that when I had it, trouble found me more often than when I didn't have it.

Although it was her job to help, I felt she made an extra effort to help me so I went to her office with one dozen roses to show my appreciation. She was out for lunch, so I waited for about twenty minutes. As I sat in the waiting area, I remembered giving thanks to God for letting me escape from this twist of fate. A vision came to me—a flashback of another twist of fate I once escaped.

I never mentioned this story to anyone in my family because I was only about nine or ten years old and the reality gave me a shock once I heard the news the next day. On that day I played basketball around the corner at the elementary school I attended. As I walked to the school, I saw a car creeping up at a slow pace with three or four kids in the car. The car pulled up on the side of me and stopped. A friend in my class was sitting in the car. He looked up to the window from the backseat. I recognized him.

"Norman, is that you?" I said.

"Yeah."

"Where you going, man?"

"We're going for a ride. You want to go?"

"I hesitated and thought about it."

"No, I'm going to shoot some ball. Do you want to go?"

They drove off and I didn't have a good feeling about this. I knew all of the boys in the car and the oldest could not have been any more than 13 or 14 years of age. The next day, Norman did not show up for school and when I returned home from school, I saw my parents secretly reading the newspaper. They were talking with very low voices and I heard the name "Norman." They put down the paper and went into another room. I passed by the chair and picked up the paper. The headlines read, "Stab her, Norman, stab her." It turns out that Norman and the neighborhood boys stabbed an old lady 72 times and raped her. When the boys were found, they were riding around in the old lady's car with several jars of pennies.

I could not help but think as I sat waiting for the public defender to return,

"What if I had gotten in that car?"

It is one thing to be punished for committing a crime that one is responsible for. There are many sitting cells today, doing time for crimes they did not commit. This is truly a twist of fate when justice doesn't prevail, and you sit with no bail. The only thing I could imagine is that's hell in a cell.

The next day I met a young lady who was in the process of moving back home to Jacksonville. This became an emergency situation, for she had no help and I was her only hope. She gave me the opportunity to make a little money and actually I needed a trip to clear my head. This was a long trip and I had some premonitions on the way back. Once I returned to Pensacola, it did not take me long to figure out that it was not the place for me.

I talked with a good friend of mine, better known as "Rushed." He gave me a little background on Jacksonville, Florida. "Jacksonville is the largest city nationwide, by land area" he said. There were better opportunities for employment in the city with room for promotion and expansion. I made up my mind that Jacksonville, Florida was the place for me. I also felt it was best for me to move to a new town and get a new start. The next move was to talk to my companion and to let her know that I was going to move where there was a better opportunity for me. Well, she didn't like the idea and we had a few words that were not so pleasant.

The last thing I had to do, but not least at all, was to talk with my love one. That was the most difficult thing to do because I felt she needed me there with her. She was an elderly lady and I had been with her for quite some time now. She knew my situation and, since the opportunity to improve my life presented itself, she supported my decision to leave. Maybe subconsciously I felt I needed her more than she needed me. I felt I was leaving the one person I loved more than anyone in this world.

I did move shortly afterwards and started a new job where opportunity was present for me in a growing city. I was in Jacksonville for about twelve years before I had this last dream. It had a profound effect on me.

I looked at Dr. Yu and continued.

In this next dream I was sitting at this love one house on her couch with her sitting next to me. I looked at her and stated with a voice of sorrow, "You must come back. This is your home." She looked at me and said nothing. She pointed to the ceiling in an upward motion and shook her head "no." Then the strangest thing happened to me, something that I never knew existed in the form this spirit was manifesting. I quickly woke up from my dream gasping for air. I tried to pull back something that rose out of my chest. It was quite strange and I did not know what it was. I realized it was a spirit, although not my own. I didn't want it to leave my body because somehow I knew the spirit to be my love one.

This was not a dream at this point. I was fully awake.

"What is it?" My friend said.

"It's was her spirit," I replied.

She's gone."

It's so strange that I knew whose spirit it was. Her spirit was beginning to rise and leave my body. I wished I were still dreaming.

I had just recently spoken this love one, possibly two weeks ago. I expected her to visit me for a while and had made plans to go and pick her up. It had been a long time since I had seen her and I was looking forward to her visit. It was so devastating to have this happen so suddenly. There were no signs, but at least I had one last chance to see her in my dream.

I sometimes wonder if my life would have been any different without my dreams. My conscience sometimes questions me on these events in my life. If I had not had a dream of leaving Pensacola to begin a new life, and if I hadn't made a conscious decision to follow my dreams, I would have always wondered what accomplishments I could have made in my life.

I sometimes wonder if it would have been on my conscience to see my friend hit by that truck. I feel that God was protecting me from the truck smashing into him and both of us falling into the oncoming traffic.

I sometimes wonder about when I heard that my other love one past from cancer of the pancreas. He was an avid, longtime smoker, and it is a sad case when it took a tragedy like this to convince me to think twice about smoking. In the same dream, I was shown the vision of him and the birth of my satellite invention.

I sometimes wonder if it is my subconscious state of mind that God has given me that helps guide and protect me from dangerous or unsafe surroundings. I have often seen beforehand the presence of threats or dangers that later occur.

I often receive warnings in my dreams and an awareness of energy around me when I am asleep.

It is hard to explain. For example, when I am asleep, I can feel the energy of a person approaching from at least twenty feet away. Whether the person may be on the other side of the door or not, I immediately awaken with a sense of awareness.

Quite often my love one, she would come to my bedroom door in the morning and awaken me for breakfast. Before she approaches the doorknob, I would sit up in my bed aware that someone was at my door. She would do this sometimes for dinner or lunch and never at the same time of day. This amazed her so that she would sometimes stand on the outside of the door and not enter. I would call out to her, I know you are at the door." Then she would walk in with a sense of amazement, and I never heard her approach.

Often a friend on the job in Jacksonville found it amazing when he could not sneak up on me when he tried. I felt his energy always within twenty feet and turned around before he was near. After that he got a kick out of trying. I don't understand this perception, but I assume everyone has it to a small degree.

I sometimes wonder whether it is my subconscious mind that made me seek a letter of deception and discover the adulterous activities of my relationship. I remember an old saying, "Let your conscience be your guide." This is easier said than done, but this is exactly what led me to my shocking discovery –I had simply followed a conscious feeling. God has given me a subconscious state of mind that may be a key to my visions and dreams.

I sometimes wonder, "Is it my subconscious mind that haunted me through one of the most difficult dreams I had?" I was planning to travel to Pensacola and take my love one to Jacksonville to visit or live with me.

I continued to have dreams after she passed on and she would appear to me quite often. The last time I saw her in this type of dream was when she appeared to me lying down with her eyes closed. Her eyes opened very quietly and I jumped in my dream in a state of anger. I said, "Don't do this to me. You are no longer here but you are always in my heart." This was the last time I saw her in these dreams.

Then Dr. Yu said, "losing a love one is always unpredictable. You had no way of knowing. It is not your fault. Life is unpredictable. Her pains and suffering are over and she's in Paradise. You will understand it better as time goes by."

Again his back was turned. He picked up his pen and wrote on his notepad the word "unpredictable" in large letters.

God continues to work with man in many
ways as he did in biblical days.

Isa 57:1

The righteous perisheth, and no man layeth it to hart:
And merciful men are taken away, none considering that
the righteous is taken away from the evil to come.

Isa 57: 2

He shell enter into peace; they shell rest in their beds, each
one walking in his uprightness.

CHAPTER 8

Well, Dr. Yu years later I met a friend who told me a story about how she met her love and his tragic departure. After she told me her story, I saw the end of her life in this dream afterwards. It was many flashes of pictures in this dream that was shown and I awakened. For these are pictures that I have envisioned are the signs of the end of time.

Soon, mankind will suffer through the most devastating, bloody war in human history called the great tribulation. Biblical scripture states, "for then there will be great tribulation, such has not been since the beginning of the world until this time, no, nor ever shall be." And unless those days were shortened, no flesh would be saved.

The Son of Man/Christ gives a series of signs that must occur before He returns. Nevertheless, we shall first hear of small wars and rumors of wars, false prophets, famines, disease, epidemics, and earthquakes. All these are the beginning of sorrow and the sound of the first and second trumpet has past.

Mt 24:1 And Jesus went out, and departed from the temple: and his disciples came to him for to show him the buildings of the temple.

Mt 24:2 And Jesus said unto them, See ye not all these things? verily I say unto you, There shall not be left here one stone upon another, that shall not be thrown down.

Mt 24:3 And as he sat upon the mount of Olives, the disciples came unto him privately, saying, Tell us, when shall these things be? and what shall be the sign of thy coming, and of the end of the world?

Mt 24:4 And Jesus answered and said unto them, Take heed that no man deceive you.

Mt 24:5 For many shall come in my name, saying, I am Christ; and shall deceive many.

Mt 24:6 And ye shall hear of wars and rumours of wars: see that ye be not troubled: for all these things must come to pass, but the end is not yet.

Mt 24:7 For nation shall rise against nation, and kingdom against kingdom: and there shall be famines, and pestilences, and earthquakes, in divers places.

Mt 24:8 All these are the beginning of sorrows.

Mt 24:9 Then shall they deliver you up to be afflicted, and shall kill you: and ye shall be hated of all nations for my name's sake.

Mt 24:10 And then shall many be offended, and shall betray one another, and shall hate one another.

Mt 24:11 And many false prophets shall rise, and shall deceive many.

Mt 24:12 And because iniquity shall abound, the love of many shall wax cold.

Mt 24:13 But he that shall endure unto the end, the same shall be saved.

Mt 24:14 And this gospel of the kingdom shall be preached in all the world for a witness unto all nations; and then shall the end come.

Mt 24:15 When ye therefore shall see the abomination of desolation, spoken of by Daniel the prophet, stand in the holy place, (whoso readeth, let him understand:)

Mt 24:16 Then let them which be in Judaea flee into the mountains:

Mt 24:17 Let him which is on the housetop not come down to take any thing out of his house:

Mt 24:18 Neither let him which is in the field return back to take his clothes.

Mt 24:19 And woe unto them that are with child, and to them that give suck in those days!

Mt 24:20 But pray ye that your flight be not in the winter, neither on the sabbath day:

Mt 24:21 For then shall be great tribulation, such as was not since the beginning of the world to this time, no, nor ever shall be.

Mt 24:22 And except those days should be shortened, there should no flesh be saved: but for the elect's sake those days shall be shortened.

Mt 24:23 Then if any man shall say unto you, Lo, here is Christ, or there; believe it not.

Mt 24:24 For there shall arise false Christs, and false prophets, and shall show great signs and wonders; insomuch that, if it were possible, they shall deceive the very elect.

Mt 24:25 Behold, I have told you before.

Mt 24:26 Wherefore if they shall say unto you, Behold, he is in the desert; go not forth: behold, he is in the secret chambers; believe it not.

Mt 24:27 For as the lightning cometh out of the east, and shineth even unto the west; so shall also the coming of the Son of man be.

Mt 24:28 For wheresoever the carcase is, there will the eagles be gathered together.

Mt 24:29 Immediately after the tribulation of those days shall the sun be darkened, and the moon shall not give her light, and the stars shall fall from heaven, and the powers of the heavens shall be shaken:

Mt 24:30 And then shall appear the sign of the Son of man in heaven: and then shall all the tribes of the earth mourn, and they shall see the Son of man coming in the clouds of heaven with power and great glory.

Mt 24:31 And he shall send his angels with a great sound of a trumpet, and they shall gather together his elect from the four winds, from one end of heaven to the other.

Mt 24:32 Now learn a parable of the fig tree; When his branch is yet tender, and putteth forth leaves, ye know that summer is nigh:

Mt 24:33 so likewise ye, when ye shall see all these things, know that it is near, even at the doors.

Mt 24:34 Verily I say unto you, This generation shall not pass, till all these things be fulfilled.

Mt 24:35 Heaven and earth shall pass away, but my words shall not pass away.

Mt 24:36 But of that day and hour knoweth no man, no, not the angels of heaven, but my Father only.

Mt 24:37 But as the days of Noe were, so shall also the coming of the Son of man be.

Mt 24:38 For as in the days that were before the flood they were eating and drinking, marrying and giving in marriage, until the day that Noe entered into the ark,

Mt 24:39 And knew not until the flood came, and took them all away; so shall also the coming of the Son of man be.

Mt 24:40 Then shall two be in the field; the one shall be taken, and the other left.

Mt 24:41 Two women shall be grinding at the mill; the one shall be taken, and the other left.

Mt 24:42 Watch therefore: for ye know not what hour your Lord doth come.

Mt 24:43 But know this, that if the goodman of the house had known in what watch the thief would come, he would have watched, and would not have suffered his house to be broken up.

Mt 24:44 Therefore be ye also ready: for in such an hour as ye think not the Son of man cometh.

Mt 24:45 Who then is a faithful and wise servant, whom his lord hath made ruler over his household, to give them meat in due season?

Mt 24:46 Blessed is that servant, whom his lord when he cometh shall find so doing.

Mt 24:47 Verily I say unto you, That he shall make him ruler over all his goods.

Mt 24:48 But and if that evil servant shall say in his heart, My lord delayeth his coming;

Mt 24:49 And shall begin to smite his fellowservants, and to eat and drink with the drunken;

Mt 24:50 The lord of that servant shall come in a day when he looketh not for him, and in an hour that he is not aware of,

Mt 24:51 And shall cut him asunder, and appoint him his portion with the hypocrites: there shall be weeping and gnashing of teeth.

World War I was the sound of the first trumpet of Revelations as the World largest explosion ball of fire killed

8.2 million and 1/3 of all grass and trees are burnt up. Nevertheless, World War II was the was the sound of the second trumpet as the mountains are cast into the sea and 1/3 of the sea becomes blood. 52 Million Died 1/3 of the creatures and ships was destroyed. The President received a call reporting, There were 105,127 ships in World War II and exactly 1/3 was destroyed.

The story of my new friend life experiences and my dream after begins in her homeland. What interested me the most was, she came from a land where 90% of Biblical prophecy will appear, in the end-times. In a collage on the outside of Pakistan, two students meet in a classroom debate section on the first day of class. The religious views of Pakistan versus Islamic are discussed.

"Today, we will discuss the different religious views of conflict that has brought destruction to a nation of people for centuries. This religious war is more prevalent than ever, and the outside world is always watching. What are your views on a never ending wall of partition between a nation of people?" Say's the instructor.

"In Islam, we express ourselves with the creation of arts and crafts. We take pride, for it is a part of our heritage." Say's Nadia.

"In Pakistan, we believe that engraving images and pictures of images is an abomination."

"Therefore, we have a right to destroy our enemies.

We are in the fight against moderate Islam." Say's Tarse.

"The radical Islam is no more than a group of barbarians, and their only care is to enforce their own laws Say's Nadia."

"Ok, that's enough. Let's control ourselves and keep an open mind when expressing our different views." Say's the Instructor.

The class bell rings, and class in dismissed. Nadia meets up with her roommate Reshema as they walk to the dorm.

"Hi, Nadia. You look a little tense. You're having a bad day."

"I don't believe that Terser. He is the most Ignorant man I have ever seen. His arrogant and pompous views really frustrate me."

"You've known the views of the radicals. Why are you now taking it so personal? Maybe there's another reason."

"Oh, please. Are you kidding me? We are totally two different people. He gets under my skin."

Nadia and Reshema arrive at their dorm room.

In the school café, Terser is sitting in the café eating lunch with friends. His classmate Ausan brings up the heated debit between Terser and Nadia.

"Terser, what was that tension between you and Nadia today? That looked more like a lovers' quarrel than a debate." Say's Ausan.

"I just follow the law of the Koran to the letter. It's all about commitment for me."

"Is it truly about commitment or tradition?"

"It's what I truly believe, and I will not be moved."

"Speaking of the enemy, look who just walked in the door." Say's Ausan.

Nadia and Reshema enter the café and walk over to the food line. They get their food and sit at a table.

"Don't look now, but at the back of the room is your debater friend. They're looking over here." Say's Resheam.

"Don't look their way. You'll just attract their attention."

"They're leaving the table. Oh no. Don't look now. They're coming this way." Say's Reshema.

Ausen and Terser turn from the exit door and in the direction of Nadia and Reshema's table.

"Come with me. I want to ask Reshema to the wedding celebration tonight." Say's Ausan.

"Do you really need me to go with you to ask her out?"

Terser follows Ausen to the table.

"Hi, Reshema, are you attending the wedding tonight?" Say's Ausen.

"It's tonight? I thought it was tomorrow." Say's Reshema.

"I now it's tonight because I am in charge of the decorations. Ms. Nadia. Will you be attending as well?" Say's Ausan.

"No! I must study for a test."

"Come on. It's the weekend; you should enjoy yourself. You have the whole weekend to complete study."

"My priorities are just that. I won't be there." Say's Nadia.

Terser looks up and shake his head as he looks at Nadia and remains silent. A special news bulletin flashes across the TV screen. The students become silent as they view the screen.

NEWS LINE

Former President Bill Clinton called a July 2000 Camp David summit, which failed to formulate a final peace agreement-underscoring the bitter truth that both Israel and the Palestinians consider Jerusalem their exclusive capital and do not want the other to have control as the France Presses reported.

FRANCE PRESSE REPORTED

As of June 2005, the war has claimed the lives of 3,703 Palestinians and claimed the lives of 1,062 Israelis since September 2000.

Now back at the dorm room, Reshema is preparing for tonight's wedding reception. Nadia is sitting on her bad reading a book.

"Nadia, do you think there will ever be peace in our nation?" Say's Reshema.

"I don't like to sound pessimistic because I truly want to keep hoping for peace. Change is always taking place. But a nation or a man who is not willing to change and stand for the batter of humanity, is not willing to except his place in life. He's an infidel." Say Nadia. "Well, speaking of change. Would you be willing to change your mind and attend the reception tonight? Please. I can't go alone."

"I want to stay. Not only that, I can't take being in the same room with Terser three times in one day."

"Oh, come on. Don't take him so personal. He won't be the only one in the building. There will be many students, and you most likely won't see him in the crowd. Beside that, you owe me, so we can just call it even."

"No, I don't have anything to wear. I have to wash, and I won't be ready in time."

"That's no excuse. I have something nice for you. Try this on for size."

Reshema and Nadia attend the wedding reception in their stunning dresses.

"It's a large crowd. There are no seats." Say's Nadia.

"We can stand over there. The view is nice on the balcony."

Terser and Ausen sit at a table with a group of male students. Ausen recognizes Reshema and Nadia walking to the balcony.

"Look, Terser. There's Reshema. I am going over to talk with her."

"Who's her friend?" Say's Terser.

"Oh my, it's Nadia." Say's Ausen.

"It can't be. Nadia always keep her head covered and wears a long dress and black shoes."

"That's strange. I've never knew she wore shoes. I don't think you paid that much attention to her." Say's Ausen.

"You should keep your friend close and your enemies closer." Say's Terser.

"Cliché! Now come, let's get closer to the enemy as well as her friend." Say's Ausen.

Terser and Ausen walks to the balcony to meet Reshema and Nadia.

"Hello, Reshema. You've arrived. You look nice. Ms Nadia, you're looking very elegant tonight. Isn't she, Terser?"

"Thank you. And how are you?" Say's Nadia.

"I'm good now that Reshema is here."

"I thought you had homework. I didn't think you would attend the event tonight. Say's Terser."

"Mr. Terser, my business shouldn't be of any concern of yours."

"Hey. Take it easy. I'm just making conversation. You really look nice tonight."

"Reshema, would you like to dance."

Ausen and Reshema walk to the dance floor with a slow dance. Terser and Nadia remain near the balcony and talk.

"Look, Nadia. Maybe we got off to a bad start. Let not our differences cause dissension between us. Let's start over and at least be civil towards one another."

Say's Terser.

Terser extends his hand.

"My name is Terser."

Nadia pauses with her arms folded. She looks at him and extends her hand.

"Hi, I'm Nadia. By the way, what you see here is not me. I often wear my hair covered and wear a long dress and conservative shoes."

"I like the conservative look. It leaves something to the imagination. By the way, it's nice to meet you and I'm not always the strong opinionated type. I am flexible and can be open-minded."

"Well, it's a pleasure to meet you, Mr. Terser."

"Would you like to dance?"

"Yes. Thank you.

Nadia and Terser walk to the dance floor. Ausen and Reshema return to the balcony.

"Where is Nadia? Say's Reshema."

"I hope Terser didn't run her away. You know, they can't be in the same room with one another for a minute with out fighting. Look, on the dance floor. Say's Reshema."

"Dancing with the enemy. Now, that's what I call keeping your enemy close." Say's Ausan.

"What are you talking about?" Say's Reshema.

"I'm just joking. They actually look good together."

Terser and Nadia walks back to the balcony with Ausan and Reshema.

"Now that we are all friends let us go and get the ladies some refreshments. Would you ladies like something to drink?" Say's Ausan.

"Yes, thank you. I would like tea, please."

"Nadia, would you like something?" Say's Terser.

"Yes. I would like the same, please."

"Ok, I'll be right back."

Terser and Ausan walks to the other end of the building to get refreshment.

"Well, I've heard of keeping the enemy close, but dancing with the enemy takes on another meaning." Say's Ausan.

"Once I got to know her, she appears to be nice. We both agreed to drop our quarrels and I'd like to know more about her."

Terser and Ausan stand at the table and talk a moment. Nadia and Reshema stand on the balcony.

"So! Has the debate ended? Have you reconciled your differences?" Say's Reshema.

"No. My feelings are the same. He doesn't seem to be so bad once he drops the male ego."

Terser and Ausan return to the balcony with Nadia and Reshema.

"Here we are ladies. Cold ice tea for everyone." Say's Ausan.

Terser and Ausan escort the girls to the dorm room. Terser and Nadia walks ahead of Ausan and Reshema.

"Did you enjoy tonight?" Say's Ausan.

"Yes, I did. I really enjoyed myself.

Is it just I, or did Nadia and Terser make a connection tonight." Say's Reshema.

"I'm more interested in the connection we made tonight. Did you feel the same fireworks between us that I felt tonight?" Say's Ausan.

"Let's not confuse fireworks with a few sparks."

"Maybe we can attend the outside festivals tomorrow."

"Yes. Then I can show you what real fireworks look like." Say's Reshema.

Terser and Nadia walks ahead.

"I really had a good time tonight. I didn't think you would be so much fun." Say's Terser.

"Why? Is it because I'm normally conservatively dressed?"

"No. I like the conservative look. It leaves something to the imagination. We never communicated on this level. It's nice and pleasant. Maybe we can do this again sometime."

"Who knows, maybe we can talk about more than just barbaric religion and politics." Says Nadia.

The next morning, Terser and Ausan are sitting eating breakfast in the school café.

"Hey, how was your night?" Say's Terser.

"My night was good, and I see you didn't have such a bad night yourself. Tonight Reshema and I will attend the festival. Will Nadia be there also?"

"Well, I did have a great time with her. I'm really beginning to feel an appreciation for her. I'm not sure if she's attending the festival."

On the next day as class is in session. The instructor continues the subject on politics and religion in Israel.

"Today class, we will continue our topic on politics and religious conflict in Israel."

Terser raises his hand.

"Yes, Mr. Terser. You have a question? Say's the instruction."

"I think my views last week may have been a little harsh. I think my views may be a reflection of my family's influence. This does not support the nature of my personal beliefs. I'm really starting to reexamine myself. I would like to apologize to Ms. Nadia and the rest of the class for my pass behavior."

"Well, Mr. Terser. That's very courageous of you. I'm sure the class accepts your apology. Now moving on."

On the same night Reshema is preparing for the festival as she receives a phone call from Ausan. "Hello. Hi, Ausan. I'm getting ready for tonight. Who's that in the background?"

"That's Terser. He asks is Nadia going to the festival?"

"Nadia. Terser asked are you going to the festival."

"I don't think I will. I have too much homework to finish."

"She won't be able to attend because she has work to complete."

Ausan arrives at the girls dorm lobby. He makes a call to her room as he sits downstairs.

"Hello. Yes, I'm getting ready. I'll be right down." Say's Reshema.

Reshema meets Ausan downstairs and they walk several blocks down to the festival. Terser is at the Festival early standing along as Ausan and Reshema recognize him from afar.

"Hey! You guys made it on time. They're just getting started. I gust Nadia decided not to come. Say's Terser."

"I couldn't pull her from the books tonight. I just couldn't persuade her."

"Well, I gust she has her priorities in order." Say's Terser.

On the night of the festival, Nadia is sitting on her bed studying. She suddenly closes her book and walks over to the closet. She pulls out her normal dress wear. She keeps her head covered and wears a long dress. Nadia pauses and views the TV as a special newsbreak appears across the screen.

The West's perception of Middle East and its relation to world terrorism was changed on September 11, 2001 when terrorists had four planes, which they used as missiles, destroying the twin towers of the World Trade Center in New York and damaging the Pentagon in Washington.

President George W. Bush has identified an "axis of evil" that includes two Middle East nations-Iran and Iraq.

"Now I will show you this evil that terrified the American nation in one Frontier of Fear."

The $20 bill is the most circulated bill to this day in America. If you go to an ATM machine today, it will give you no other bill than a 20. Sometimes in over lives we hold the future in our hands and don't know it's there. But beware.

1 Timothy 6:9-10 but they that will be rich fall into temptation and a snare, and into many foolish and hurtful lust, which drown men in destruction and perdition. For the love of money is the root of all evil: which while some coveted after, they have erred from the faith, and pierced themselves through with many sorrows.

It's scriptural that the love of money is the root of all evil. Just take a $ 20 bill. Fold a $20 bill in half.

Half $20 bill

Fold again as below.

Fold up $20

Fold the other end up, exactly as before.

Picture Of Pentagon on Fire.

It reveals a picture of the Pentagon on fire.

It reveals a picture of the Twin Towers on fire.

Now turn it over.

Fold half $20

Now fold an open $20 bill facing the back as shown.

It reveals a picture of OSAMA name as shown.

There's a triple coincidence on a $20 bill that's been reveal sense the beginning of it's creation that is associated with **9-11**.

Disaster (Twin Towers)

Disaster (Pentagon)

Disaster (Osama)

Last, but not less. 9 + 11 = 20

In the Book of Isaiah:30: 25-26: And there shell be upon every high mountain, and upon every high hill; rivers and stream of waters in the day of the great slaughter, when the towers fall. Isa:26- Moreover the light of the moon shell be as the light of the sun, and the light of the sun sevenfold, as the light of seen days, in the day that the Lord bindeth up the branches of his people; and healeth the smoke of their wound.

Isaiah: 30.9:10 "The brick having falling, but we will rebuild with cut stones; the sycamores have been cut down, but we will replace them with Cedars"09/11/2001 -WTC towers hit by planes and fell to the ground.

-A sycamore tree struck down by debris from the last tower to fall is retrieved and made into a sign called "The Sycamore of ground zero"

-Senate Majority Leader Tom Daschie at Capital Hills says, "America will emerge from this tragedy as we have emerged from all adversity- untied and strong....-"

And quotes Isaiah 9-10 about rebuilding and recovering.

09/28/2001 -Sock market crash(684points)

11-22-2003 -Norway Spruce "Tree of hope" is planted at ground zero, replacing the lost sycamore.

- 07/04/2004 - A 20 ton stone quarried from upper state New York is installed at ground Zero with a ceremony on The nation declares then "We will rebuild"
- 09/11/2004- Presidential candidate John Edwards, Quotes Isaiah 09-10 about rebuilding in a speech in Washington, DC on the third anniversary of 9/11.
- 4/27/2006 - America rebuilds on Ground zero(**Freedom Tower** breaks ground)
- 09/29.2008 - Stock market crash(777points) Don't underestimate the year 2020 in the corner of the bill. This very Significant in future biblical Prophecy.

2020

Shell we look upon this year in time of peace, or destruction. It is of holly truth, a people of God the Lord and saver" Christ" was born into the world and brought salvation to all man. A new birth shell appear in the latter days to bring deception and destruction of the number of a man 666.

Daniel 1

1 In the third year of the reign of Jehoiakim king of Judah came Nebuchadnezzar king of Babylon unto Jerusalem, and besieged it.

2 And the Lord gave Jehoiakim king of Judah into his hand, with part of the vessels of the house of God: which he carried into the land of Shinar to the house of his god; and he brought the vessels into the treasure house of his god.

3 And the king spake unto Ashpenaz the master of his eunuchs, that he should bring certain of the children of Israel, and of the king's seed, and of the princes;

4 Children in whom was no blemish, but well favoured, and skilful in all wisdom, and cunning in knowledge, and understanding science, and such as had ability in them to stand in the king's palace, and whom they might teach the learning and the tongue of the Chaldeans.

5 And the king appointed them a daily provision of the king's meat, and of the wine which he drank: so nourishing them three years, that at the end thereof they might stand before the king.

6 Now among these were of the children of Judah, Daniel, Hananiah, Mishael, and Azariah:

7 Unto whom the prince of the eunuchs gave names: for he gave unto Daniel the name of Belteshazzar; and to Hananiah, of Shadrach; and to Mishael, of Meshach; and to Azariah, of Abednego.

8 But Daniel purposed in his heart that he would not defile himself with the portion of the king's meat, nor with the wine which he drank: therefore he requested of the prince of the eunuchs that he might not defile himself.

9 Now God had brought Daniel into favour and tender love with the prince of the eunuchs.

10 And the prince of the eunuchs said unto Daniel, I fear my lord the king, who hath appointed your meat and your drink: for why should he see your faces worse liking than the children which are of your sort? then shall ye make me endanger my head to the king.

11 Then said Daniel to Melzar, whom the prince of the eunuchs had set over Daniel, Hananiah, Mishael, and Azariah,

12 Prove thy servants, I beseech thee, ten days; and let them give us pulse to eat, and water to drink.

13 Then let our countenances be looked upon before thee, and the countenance of the children that eat of the portion of the king's meat: and as thou seest, deal with thy servants.

14 So he consented to them in this matter, and proved them ten days.

15 And at the end of ten days their countenances appeared fairer and fatter in flesh than all the children which did eat the portion of the king's meat.

16 Thus Melzar took away the portion of their meat, and the wine that they should drink; and gave them pulse.

17 As for these four children, God gave them knowledge and skill in all learning and wisdom: and Daniel had understanding in all visions and dreams.

18 Now at the end of the days that the king had said he should bring them in, then the prince of the eunuchs brought them in before Nebuchadnezzar.

19 And the king communed with them; and among them all was found none like Daniel, Hananiah, Mishael, and Azariah: therefore stood they before the king.

20 And in all matters of wisdom and understanding, that the king enquired of them, he found them ten times better than all the magicians and astrologers that were in all his realm.

21 And Daniel continued even unto the first year of king Cyrus.

Daniel 2

1 And in the second year of the reign of Nebuchadnezzar Nebuchadnezzar dreamed dreams, wherewith his spirit was troubled, and his sleep brake from him.

2 Then the king commanded to call the magicians, and the astrologers, and the sorcerers, and the Chaldeans, for to shew the king his dreams. So they came and stood before the king.

3 And the king said unto them, I have dreamed a dream, and my spirit was troubled to know the dream.

4 Then spake the Chaldeans to the king in Syriack, O king, live for ever: tell thy servants the dream, and we will shew the interpretation.

5 The king answered and said to the Chaldeans, The thing is gone from me: if ye will not make known unto me the dream, with the interpretation thereof, ye shall be cut in pieces, and your houses shall be made a dunghill.

6 But if ye shew the dream, and the interpretation thereof, ye shall receive of me gifts and rewards and great honour: therefore shew me the dream, and the interpretation thereof.

7 They answered again and said, Let the king tell his servants the dream, and we will shew the interpretation of it.

8 The king answered and said, I know of certainty that ye would gain the time, because ye see the thing is gone from me.

9 But if ye will not make known unto me the dream, there is but one decree for you: for ye have prepared lying and corrupt words to speak before me, till the time be changed: therefore tell me the dream, and I shall know that ye can shew me the interpretation thereof.

10 The Chaldeans answered before the king, and said, There is not a man upon the earth that can shew the king's matter: therefore there is no king, lord, nor ruler, that asked such things at any magician, or astrologer, or Chaldean.

11 And it is a rare thing that the king requireth, and there is none other that can shew it before the king, except the gods, whose dwelling is not with flesh.

12 For this cause the king was angry and very furious, and commanded to destroy all the wise men of Babylon.

13 And the decree went forth that the wise men should be slain; and they sought Daniel and his fellows to be slain.

14 Then Daniel answered with counsel and wisdom to Arioch the captain of the king's guard, which was gone forth to slay the wise men of Babylon:

15 He answered and said to Arioch the king's captain, Why is the decree so hasty from the king? Then Arioch made the thing known to Daniel.

16 Then Daniel went in, and desired of the king that he would give him time, and that he would shew the king the interpretation.

17 Then Daniel went to his house, and made the thing known to Hananiah, Mishael, and Azariah, his companions:

18 That they would desire mercies of the God of heaven concerning this secret; that Daniel and his fellows should not perish with the rest of the wise men of Babylon.

19 Then was the secret revealed unto Daniel in a night vision. Then Daniel blessed the God of heaven.

20 Daniel answered and said, Blessed be the name of God for ever and ever: for wisdom and might are his:

21 And he changeth the times and the seasons: he removeth kings, and setteth up kings: he giveth wisdom unto the wise, and knowledge to them that know understanding:

22 He revealeth the deep and secret things: he knoweth what is in the darkness, and the light dwelleth with him.

23 I thank thee, and praise thee, O thou God of my fathers, who hast given me wisdom and might, and hast made known unto me now what we desired of thee: for thou hast now made known unto us the king's matter.

24 Therefore Daniel went in unto Arioch, whom the king had ordained to destroy the wise men of Babylon: he went and said thus unto him; Destroy not the wise men of Babylon: bring me in before the king, and I will shew unto the king the interpretation.

25 Then Arioch brought in Daniel before the king in haste, and said thus unto him, I have found a man of the captives of Judah, that will make known unto the king the interpretation.

26 The king answered and said to Daniel, whose name was Belteshazzar, Art thou able to make known unto me the dream which I have seen, and the interpretation thereof?

27 Daniel answered in the presence of the king, and said, The secret which the king hath demanded cannot the wise men, the astrologers, the magicians, the soothsayers, shew unto the king;

28 But there is a God in heaven that revealeth secrets, and maketh known to the king Nebuchadnezzar what shall be in the latter days. Thy dream, and the visions of thy head upon thy bed, are these;

29 As for thee, O king, thy thoughts came into thy mind upon thy bed, what should come to pass hereafter: and he that revealeth secrets maketh known to thee what shall come to pass.

30 But as for me, this secret is not revealed to me for any wisdom that I have more than any living, but for their sakes that shall make known the interpretation to the king, and that thou mightest know the thoughts of thy heart.

31 Thou, O king, sawest, and behold a great image. This great image, whose brightness was excellent, stood before thee; and the form thereof was terrible.

32 This image's head was of fine gold, his breast and his arms of silver, his belly and his thighs of brass,

33 His legs of iron, his feet part of iron and part of clay.

34 Thou sawest till that a stone was cut out without hands, which smote the image upon his feet that were of iron and clay, and brake them to pieces.

35 Then was the iron, the clay, the brass, the silver, and the gold, broken to pieces together, and became like the chaff of the summer threshingfloors; and the wind carried them away, that no place was found for them: and the stone that smote the image became a great mountain, and filled the whole earth.

36 This is the dream; and we will tell the interpretation thereof before the king.

37 Thou, O king, art a king of kings: for the God of heaven hath given thee a kingdom, power, and strength, and glory.

38 And wheresoever the children of men dwell, the beasts of the field and the fowls of the heaven hath he given into thine hand, and hath made thee ruler over them all. Thou art this head of gold.

39 And after thee shall arise another kingdom inferior to thee, and another third kingdom of brass, which shall bear rule over all the earth.

40 And the fourth kingdom shall be strong as iron: forasmuch as iron breaketh in pieces and subdueth all things: and as iron that breaketh all these, shall it break in pieces and bruise.

41 And whereas thou sawest the feet and toes, part of potters' clay, and part of iron, the kingdom shall be divided; but there

shall be in it of the strength of the iron, forasmuch as thou sawest the iron mixed with miry clay.

42 And as the toes of the feet were part of iron, and part of clay, so the kingdom shall be partly strong, and partly broken.

43 And whereas thou sawest iron mixed with miry clay, they shall mingle themselves with the seed of men: but they shall not cleave one to another, even as iron is not mixed with clay.

44 And in the days of these kings shall the God of heaven set up a kingdom, which shall never be destroyed: and the kingdom shall not be left to other people, but it shall break in pieces and consume all these kingdoms, and it shall stand for ever.

45 Forasmuch as thou sawest that the stone was cut out of the mountain without hands, and that it brake in pieces the iron, the brass, the clay, the silver, and the gold; the great God hath made known to the king what shall come to pass hereafter: and the dream is certain, and the interpretation thereof sure.

46 Then the king Nebuchadnezzar fell upon his face, and worshipped Daniel, and commanded that they should offer an oblation and sweet odours unto him.

47 The king answered unto Daniel, and said, Of a truth it is, that your God is a God of gods, and a Lord of kings, and a revealer of secrets, seeing thou couldest reveal this secret.

48 Then the king made Daniel a great man, and gave him many great gifts, and made him ruler over the whole province of Babylon, and chief of the governors over all the wise men of Babylon.

49 Then Daniel requested of the king, and he set Shadrach, Meshach, and Abednego, over the affairs of the province of Babylon: but Daniel sat in the gate of the king.

Daniel 3

1 Nebuchadnezzar the king made an image of gold, whose height was threescore cubits, and the breadth thereof six cubits: he set it up in the plain of Dura, in the province of Babylon.

2 Then Nebuchadnezzar the king sent to gather together the princes, the governors, and the captains, the judges, the treasurers, the counsellors, the sheriffs, and all the rulers of the provinces, to come to the dedication of the image which Nebuchadnezzar the king had set up.

3 Then the princes, the governors, and captains, the judges, the treasurers, the counsellors, the sheriffs, and all the rulers of the provinces, were gathered together unto the dedication of the image that Nebuchadnezzar the king had set up; and they stood before the image that Nebuchadnezzar had set up.

4 Then an herald cried aloud, To you it is commanded, O people, nations, and languages,

5 That at what time ye hear the sound of the cornet, flute, harp, sackbut, psaltery, dulcimer, and all kinds of musick, ye fall down and worship the golden image that Nebuchadnezzar the king hath set up:

6 And whoso falleth not down and worshippeth shall the same hour be cast into the midst of a burning fiery furnace.

7 Therefore at that time, when all the people heard the sound of the cornet, flute, harp, sackbut, psaltery, and all kinds of musick, all the people, the nations, and the languages, fell down and worshipped the golden image that Nebuchadnezzar the king had set up.

8 Wherefore at that time certain Chaldeans came near, and accused the Jews.

9 They spake and said to the king Nebuchadnezzar, O king, live for ever.

10 Thou, O king, hast made a decree, that every man that shall hear the sound of the cornet, flute, harp, sackbut, psaltery, and dulcimer, and all kinds of musick, shall fall down and worship the golden image:

11 And whoso falleth not down and worshippeth, that he should be cast into the midst of a burning fiery furnace.

12 There are certain Jews whom thou hast set over the affairs of the province of Babylon, Shadrach, Meshach, and Abednego; these men, O king, have not regarded thee: they serve not thy gods, nor worship the golden image which thou hast set up.

13 Then Nebuchadnezzar in his rage and fury commanded to bring Shadrach, Meshach, and Abednego. Then they brought these men before the king.

14 Nebuchadnezzar spake and said unto them, Is it true, O Shadrach, Meshach, and Abednego, do not ye serve my gods, nor worship the golden image which I have set up?

15 Now if ye be ready that at what time ye hear the sound of the cornet, flute, harp, sackbut, psaltery, and dulcimer, and all kinds of musick, ye fall down and worship the image which I have made; well: but if ye worship not, ye shall be cast the same hour into the midst of a burning fiery furnace; and who is that God that shall deliver you out of my hands?

16 Shadrach, Meshach, and Abednego, answered and said to the king, O Nebuchadnezzar, we are not careful to answer thee in this matter.

17 If it be so, our God whom we serve is able to deliver us from the burning fiery furnace, and he will deliver us out of thine hand, O king.

18 But if not, be it known unto thee, O king, that we will not serve thy gods, nor worship the golden image which thou hast set up.

19 Then was Nebuchadnezzar full of fury, and the form of his visage was changed against Shadrach, Meshach, and Abednego: therefore he spake, and commanded that they should heat the furnace one seven times more than it was wont to be heated.

20 And he commanded the most mighty men that were in his army to bind Shadrach, Meshach, and Abednego, and to cast them into the burning fiery furnace.

21 Then these men were bound in their coats, their hosen, and their hats, and their other garments, and were cast into the midst of the burning fiery furnace.

22 Therefore because the king's commandment was urgent, and the furnace exceeding hot, the flames of the fire slew those men that took up Shadrach, Meshach, and Abednego.

23 And these three men, Shadrach, Meshach, and Abednego, fell down bound into the midst of the burning fiery furnace.

24 Then Nebuchadnezzar the king was astonished, and rose up in haste, and spake, and said unto his counsellors, Did not we cast three men bound into the midst of the fire? They answered and said unto the king, True, O king.

25 He answered and said, Lo, I see four men loose, walking in the midst of the fire, and they have no hurt; and the form of the fourth is like the Son of God.

26 Then Nebuchadnezzar came near to the mouth of the burning fiery furnace, and spake, and said, Shadrach, Meshach, and Abednego, ye servants of the most high God, come forth, and come hither. Then Shadrach, Meshach, and Abednego, came forth of the midst of the fire.

27 And the princes, governors, and captains, and the king's counsellors, being gathered together, saw these men, upon whose bodies the fire had no power, nor was an hair of their head singed, neither were their coats changed, nor the smell of fire had passed on them.

28 Then Nebuchadnezzar spake, and said, Blessed be the God of Shadrach, Meshach, and Abednego, who hath sent his angel, and delivered his servants that trusted in him, and have changed the king's word, and yielded their bodies, that they might not serve nor worship any god, except their own God.

29 Therefore I make a decree, That every people, nation, and language, which speak any thing amiss against the God of Shadrach, Meshach, and Abednego, shall be cut in pieces, and their houses shall be made a dunghill: because there is no other God that can deliver after this sort.

30 Then the king promoted Shadrach, Meshach, and Abednego, in the province of Babylon.

Daniel 4

1 Nebuchadnezzar the king, unto all people, nations, and languages, that dwell in all the earth; Peace be multiplied unto you.

2 I thought it good to shew the signs and wonders that the high God hath wrought toward me.

3 How great are his signs! and how mighty are his wonders! his kingdom is an everlasting kingdom, and his dominion is from generation to generation.

4 I Nebuchadnezzar was at rest in mine house, and flourishing in my palace:

5 I saw a dream which made me afraid, and the thoughts upon my bed and the visions of my head troubled me.

6 Therefore made I a decree to bring in all the wise men of Babylon before me, that they might make known unto me the interpretation of the dream.

7 Then came in the magicians, the astrologers, the Chaldeans, and the soothsayers: and I told the dream before them; but they did not make known unto me the interpretation thereof.

8 But at the last Daniel came in before me, whose name was Belteshazzar, according to the name of my God, and in whom is the spirit of the holy gods: and before him I told the dream, saying,

9 O Belteshazzar, master of the magicians, because I know that the spirit of the holy gods is in thee, and no secret troubleth thee, tell me the visions of my dream that I have seen, and the interpretation thereof.

10 Thus were the visions of mine head in my bed; I saw, and behold a tree in the midst of the earth, and the height thereof was great.

11 The tree grew, and was strong, and the height thereof reached unto heaven, and the sight thereof to the end of all the earth:

12 The leaves thereof were fair, and the fruit thereof much, and in it was meat for all: the beasts of the field had shadow under it, and the fowls of the heaven dwelt in the boughs thereof, and all flesh was fed of it.

13 I saw in the visions of my head upon my bed, and, behold, a watcher and an holy one came down from heaven;

14 He cried aloud, and said thus, Hew down the tree, and cut off his branches, shake off his leaves, and scatter his fruit: let the beasts get away from under it, and the fowls from his branches:

15 Nevertheless leave the stump of his roots in the earth, even with a band of iron and brass, in the tender grass of the field; and let it be wet with the dew of heaven, and let his portion be with the beasts in the grass of the earth:

16 Let his heart be changed from man's, and let a beast's heart be given unto him; and let seven times pass over him.

17 This matter is by the decree of the watchers, and the demand by the word of the holy ones: to the intent that the living may know that the most High ruleth in the kingdom of men, and giveth it to whomsoever he will, and setteth up over it the basest of men.

18 This dream I king Nebuchadnezzar have seen. Now thou, O Belteshazzar, declare the interpretation thereof, forasmuch as all the wise men of my kingdom are not able to make known unto me the interpretation: but thou art able; for the spirit of the holy gods is in thee.

19 Then Daniel, whose name was Belteshazzar, was astonied for one hour, and his thoughts troubled him. The king spake, and said, Belteshazzar, let not the dream, or the interpretation thereof, trouble thee. Belteshazzar answered and said, My lord, the dream be to them that hate thee, and the interpretation thereof to thine enemies.

20 The tree that thou sawest, which grew, and was strong, whose height reached unto the heaven, and the sight thereof to all the earth;

21 Whose leaves were fair, and the fruit thereof much, and in it was meat for all; under which the beasts of the field dwelt, and upon whose branches the fowls of the heaven had their habitation:

22 It is thou, O king, that art grown and become strong: for thy greatness is grown, and reacheth unto heaven, and thy dominion to the end of the earth.

23 And whereas the king saw a watcher and an holy one coming down from heaven, and saying, Hew the tree down, and destroy it; yet leave the stump of the roots thereof in the earth, even with a band of iron and brass, in the tender grass of the field; and let it be wet with the dew of heaven, and let his portion be with the beasts of the field, till seven times pass over him;

24 This is the interpretation, O king, and this is the decree of the most High, which is come upon my lord the king:

25 That they shall drive thee from men, and thy dwelling shall be with the beasts of the field, and they shall make thee to eat grass as oxen, and they shall wet thee with the dew of heaven, and seven times shall pass over thee, till thou know that the most High ruleth in the kingdom of men, and giveth it to whomsoever he will.

26 And whereas they commanded to leave the stump of the tree roots; thy kingdom shall be sure unto thee, after that thou shalt have known that the heavens do rule.

27 Wherefore, O king, let my counsel be acceptable unto thee, and break off thy sins by righteousness, and thine iniquities by shewing mercy to the poor; if it may be a lengthening of thy tranquillity.

28 All this came upon the king Nebuchadnezzar.

29 At the end of twelve months he walked in the palace of the kingdom of Babylon.

30 The king spake, and said, Is not this great Babylon, that I have built for the house of the kingdom by the might of my power, and for the honour of my majesty?

31 While the word was in the king's mouth, there fell a voice from heaven, saying, O king Nebuchadnezzar, to thee it is spoken; The kingdom is departed from thee.

32 And they shall drive thee from men, and thy dwelling shall be with the beasts of the field: they shall make thee to eat grass as oxen, and seven times shall pass over thee, until thou know that the most High ruleth in the kingdom of men, and giveth it to whomsoever he will.

33 The same hour was the thing fulfilled upon Nebuchadnezzar: and he was driven from men, and did eat grass as oxen, and his body was wet with the dew of heaven, till his hairs were grown like eagles' feathers, and his nails like birds' claws.

34 And at the end of the days I Nebuchadnezzar lifted up mine eyes unto heaven, and mine understanding returned unto me, and I blessed the most High, and I praised and honored him that liveth for ever, whose dominion is an everlasting dominion, and his kingdom is from generation to generation:

35 And all the inhabitants of the earth are reputed as nothing: and he doeth according to his will in the army of heaven, and among the inhabitants of the earth: and none can stay his hand, or say unto him, What doest thou?

36 At the same time my reason returned unto me; and for the glory of my kingdom, mine honour and brightness returned unto me; and my counsellors and my lords sought unto me; and I was established in my kingdom, and excellent majesty was added unto me.

37 Now I Nebuchadnezzar praise and extol and honour the King of heaven, all whose works are truth, and his ways judgment: and those that walk in pride he is able to abase.

Daniel 5

1 Belshazzar the king made a great feast to a thousand of his lords, and drank wine before the thousand.

2 Belshazzar, whiles he tasted the wine, commanded to bring the golden and silver vessels which his father Nebuchadnezzar had taken out of the temple which was in Jerusalem; that the king, and his princes, his wives, and his concubines, might drink therein.

3 Then they brought the golden vessels that were taken out of the temple of the house of God which was at Jerusalem; and the king, and his princes, his wives, and his concubines, drank in them.

4 They drank wine, and praised the gods of gold, and of silver, of brass, of iron, of wood, and of stone.

5 In the same hour came forth fingers of a man's hand, and wrote over against the candlestick upon the plaister of the wall of the king's palace: and the king saw the part of the hand that wrote.

6 Then the king's countenance was changed, and his thoughts troubled him, so that the joints of his loins were loosed, and his knees smote one against another.

7 The king cried aloud to bring in the astrologers, the Chaldeans, and the soothsayers. And the king spake, and said to the wise men of Babylon, Whosoever shall read this writing, and shew me the interpretation thereof, shall be clothed with scarlet, and have a chain of gold about his neck, and shall be the third ruler in the kingdom.

8 Then came in all the king's wise men: but they could not read the writing, nor make known to the king the interpretation thereof.

9 Then was king Belshazzar greatly troubled, and his countenance was changed in him, and his lords were astonied.

10 Now the queen by reason of the words of the king and his lords came into the banquet house: and the queen spake and said, O king, live for ever: let not thy thoughts trouble thee, nor let thy countenance be changed:

11 There is a man in thy kingdom, in whom is the spirit of the holy gods; and in the days of thy father light and understanding and wisdom, like the wisdom of the gods, was found in him; whom the king Nebuchadnezzar thy father, the king, I say, thy father, made master of the magicians, astrologers, Chaldeans, and soothsayers;

12 Forasmuch as an excellent spirit, and knowledge, and understanding, interpreting of dreams, and shewing of hard sentences, and dissolving of doubts, were found in the same Daniel, whom the king named Belteshazzar: now let Daniel be called, and he will shew the interpretation.

13 Then was Daniel brought in before the king. And the king spake and said unto Daniel, Art thou that Daniel, which art of the children of the captivity of Judah, whom the king my father brought out of Jewry?

14 I have even heard of thee, that the spirit of the gods is in thee, and that light and understanding and excellent wisdom is found in thee.

15 And now the wise men, the astrologers, have been brought in before me, that they should read this writing, and make known unto me the interpretation thereof: but they could not shew the interpretation of the thing:

16 And I have heard of thee, that thou canst make interpretations, and dissolve doubts: now if thou canst read the writing, and make known to me the interpretation thereof, thou shalt be clothed with scarlet, and have a chain of gold about thy neck, and shalt be the third ruler in the kingdom.

17 Then Daniel answered and said before the king, Let thy gifts be to thyself, and give thy rewards to another; yet I will read the writing unto the king, and make known to him the interpretation.

18 O thou king, the most high God gave Nebuchadnezzar thy father a kingdom, and majesty, and glory, and honour:

19 And for the majesty that he gave him, all people, nations, and languages, trembled and feared before him: whom he would he slew; and whom he would he kept alive; and whom he would he set up; and whom he would he put down.

20 But when his heart was lifted up, and his mind hardened in pride, he was deposed from his kingly throne, and they took his glory from him:

21 And he was driven from the sons of men; and his heart was made like the beasts, and his dwelling was with the wild asses: they fed him with grass like oxen, and his body was wet with the dew of heaven; till he knew that the most high God

ruled in the kingdom of men, and that he appointeth over it whomsoever he will.

22 And thou his son, O Belshazzar, hast not humbled thine heart, though thou knewest all this;

23 But hast lifted up thyself against the Lord of heaven; and they have brought the vessels of his house before thee, and thou, and thy lords, thy wives, and thy concubines, have drunk wine in them; and thou hast praised the gods of silver, and gold, of brass, iron, wood, and stone, which see not, nor hear, nor know: and the God in whose hand thy breath is, and whose are all thy ways, hast thou not glorified:

24 Then was the part of the hand sent from him; and this writing was written.

25 And this is the writing that was written, MENE, MENE, TEKEL, UPHARSIN.

26 This is the interpretation of the thing: MENE; God hath numbered thy kingdom, and finished it.

27 TEKEL; Thou art weighed in the balances, and art found wanting.

28 PERES; Thy kingdom is divided, and given to the Medes and Persians.

29 Then commanded Belshazzar, and they clothed Daniel with scarlet, and put a chain of gold about his neck, and made a proclamation concerning him, that he should be the third ruler in the kingdom.

30 In that night was Belshazzar the king of the Chaldeans slain.

31 And Darius the Median took the kingdom, being about threescore and two years old.

Daniel 6

1 It pleased Darius to set over the kingdom an hundred and twenty princes, which should be over the whole kingdom;

2 And over these three presidents; of whom Daniel was first: that the princes might give accounts unto them, and the king should have no damage.

3 Then this Daniel was preferred above the presidents and princes, because an excellent spirit was in him; and the king thought to set him over the whole realm.

4 Then the presidents and princes sought to find occasion against Daniel concerning the kingdom; but they could find none occasion nor fault; forasmuch as he was faithful, neither was there any error or fault found in him.

5 Then said these men, We shall not find any occasion against this Daniel, except we find it against him concerning the law of his God.

6 Then these presidents and princes assembled together to the king, and said thus unto him, King Darius, live for ever.

7 All the presidents of the kingdom, the governors, and the princes, the counsellors, and the captains, have consulted together to establish a royal statute, and to make a firm decree, that whosoever shall ask a petition of any God or man for thirty days, save of thee, O king, he shall be cast into the den of lions.

8 Now, O king, establish the decree, and sign the writing, that it be not changed, according to the law of the Medes and Persians, which altereth not.

9 Wherefore king Darius signed the writing and the decree.

10 Now when Daniel knew that the writing was signed, he went into his house; and his windows being open in his chamber toward Jerusalem, he kneeled upon his knees three times a day, and prayed, and gave thanks before his God, as he did aforetime.

11 Then these men assembled, and found Daniel praying and making supplication before his God.

12 Then they came near, and spake before the king concerning the king's decree; Hast thou not signed a decree, that every man that shall ask a petition of any God or man within thirty days, save of thee, O king, shall be cast into the den of lions? The king answered and said, The thing is true, according to the law of the Medes and Persians, which altereth not.

13 Then answered they and said before the king, That Daniel, which is of the children of the captivity of Judah, regardeth not thee, O king, nor the decree that thou hast signed, but maketh his petition three times a day.

14 Then the king, when he heard these words, was sore displeased with himself, and set his heart on Daniel to deliver him: and he laboured till the going down of the sun to deliver him.

15 Then these men assembled unto the king, and said unto the king, Know, O king, that the law of the Medes and Persians is, That no decree nor statute which the king establisheth may be changed.

16 Then the king commanded, and they brought Daniel, and cast him into the den of lions. Now the king spake and said unto Daniel, Thy God whom thou servest continually, he will deliver thee.

17 And a stone was brought, and laid upon the mouth of the den; and the king sealed it with his own signet, and with the signet of his lords; that the purpose might not be changed concerning Daniel.

18 Then the king went to his palace, and passed the night fasting: neither were instruments of musick brought before him: and his sleep went from him.

19 Then the king arose very early in the morning, and went in haste unto the den of lions.

20 And when he came to the den, he cried with a lamentable voice unto Daniel: and the king spake and said to Daniel, O Daniel, servant of the living God, is thy God, whom thou servest continually, able to deliver thee from the lions?

21 Then said Daniel unto the king, O king, live for ever.

22 My God hath sent his angel, and hath shut the lions' mouths, that they have not hurt me: forasmuch as before him innocency was found in me; and also before thee, O king, have I done no hurt.

23 Then was the king exceedingly glad for him, and commanded that they should take Daniel up out of the den. So Daniel was taken up out of the den, and no manner of hurt was found upon him, because he believed in his God.

24 And the king commanded, and they brought those men which had accused Daniel, and they cast them into the den of lions, them, their children, and their wives; and the lions had the mastery of them, and brake all their bones in pieces or ever they came at the bottom of the den.

25 Then king Darius wrote unto all people, nations, and languages, that dwell in all the earth; Peace be multiplied unto you.

26 I make a decree, That in every dominion of my kingdom men tremble and fear before the God of Daniel: for he is the living God, and stedfast for ever, and his kingdom that which shall not be destroyed, and his dominion shall be even unto the end.

27 He delivereth and rescueth, and he worketh signs and wonders in heaven and in earth, who hath delivered Daniel from the power of the lions.

28 So this Daniel prospered in the reign of Darius, and in the reign of Cyrus the Persian.

Daniel 7

1 In the first year of Belshazzar king of Babylon Daniel had a dream and visions of his head upon his bed: then he wrote the dream, and told the sum of the matters.

2Daniel spake and said, I saw in my vision by night, and, behold, the four winds of the heaven strove upon the great sea.

3And four great beasts came up from the sea, diverse one from another.

4The first was like a lion, and had eagle's wings: I beheld till the wings thereof were plucked, and it was lifted up from the earth, and made stand upon the feet as a man, and a man's heart was given to it.

5 And behold another beast, a second, like to a bear, and it raised up itself on one side, and it had three ribs in the mouth of it between the teeth of it: and they said thus unto it, Arise, devour much flesh.

6 After this I beheld, and lo another, like a leopard, which had upon the back of it four wings of a fowl; the beast had also four heads; and dominion was given to it.

7 After this I saw in the night visions, and behold a fourth beast, dreadful and terrible, and strong exceedingly; and it had great iron teeth: it devoured and brake in pieces, and stamped the residue with the feet of it: and it was diverse from all the beasts that were before it; and it had ten horns.

8 I considered the horns, and, behold, there came up among them another little horn, before whom there were three of the first

horns plucked up by the roots: and, behold, in this horn were eyes like the eyes of man, and a mouth speaking great things.

9 I beheld till the thrones were cast down, and the Ancient of days did sit, whose garment was white as snow, and the hair of his head like the pure wool: his throne was like the fiery flame, and his wheels as burning fire.

10 A fiery stream issued and came forth from before him: thousand thousands ministered unto him, and ten thousand times ten thousand stood before him: the judgment was set, and the books were opened.

11 I beheld then because of the voice of the great words which the horn spake: I beheld even till the beast was slain, and his body destroyed, and given to the burning flame.

12 As concerning the rest of the beasts, they had their dominion taken away: yet their lives were prolonged for a season and time.

13 I saw in the night visions, and, behold, one like the Son of man came with the clouds of heaven, and came to the Ancient of days, and they brought him near before him.

14 And there was given him dominion, and glory, and a kingdom, that all people, nations, and languages, should serve him: his dominion is an everlasting dominion, which

shall not pass away, and his kingdom that which shall not be destroyed.

15 I Daniel was grieved in my spirit in the midst of my body, and the visions of my head troubled me.

16 I came near unto one of them that stood by, and asked him the truth of all this. So he told me, and made me know the interpretation of the things.

17 These great beasts, which are four, are four kings, which shall arise out of the earth.

18 But the saints of the most High shall take the kingdom, and possess the kingdom for ever, even for ever and ever.

19 Then I would know the truth of the fourth beast, which was diverse from all the others, exceeding dreadful, whose teeth were of iron, and his nails of brass; which devoured, brake in pieces, and stamped the residue with his feet;

20 And of the ten horns that were in his head, and of the other which came up, and before whom three fell; even of that horn that had eyes, and a mouth that spake very great things, whose look was more stout than his fellows.

21 I beheld, and the same horn made war with the saints, and prevailed against them;

22 Until the Ancient of days came, and judgment was given to the saints of the most High; and the time came that the saints possessed the kingdom.

23 Thus he said, The fourth beast shall be the fourth kingdom upon earth, which shall be diverse from all kingdoms, and shall devour the whole earth, and shall tread it down, and break it in pieces.

24 And the ten horns out of this kingdom are ten kings that shall arise: and another shall rise after them; and he shall be diverse from the first, and he shall subdue three kings.

25 And he shall speak great words against the most High, and shall wear out the saints of the most High, and think to change times and laws: and they shall be given into his hand until a time and times and the dividing of time.

26 But the judgment shall sit, and they shall take away his dominion, to consume and to destroy it unto the end.

27 And the kingdom and dominion, and the greatness of the kingdom under the whole heaven, shall be given to the people of the saints of the most High, whose kingdom is an everlasting kingdom, and all dominions shall serve and obey him.

28 Hitherto is the end of the matter. As for me Daniel, my cogitations much troubled me, and my countenance changed in me: but I kept the matter in my heart.

Daniel 8

1 In the third year of the reign of king Belshazzar a vision appeared unto me, even unto me Daniel, after that which appeared unto me at the first.

2 And I saw in a vision; and it came to pass, when I saw, that I was at Shushan in the palace, which is in the province of Elam; and I saw in a vision, and I was by the river of Ulai.

3Then I lifted up mine eyes, and saw, and, behold, there stood before the river a ram which had two horns: and the two horns were high; but one was higher than the other, and the higher came up last.

4I saw the ram pushing westward, and northward, and southward; so that no beasts might stand before him, neither was there any that could deliver out of his hand; but he did according to his will, and became great.

5 And as I was considering, behold, an he goat came from the west on the face of the whole earth, and touched not the ground: and the goat had a notable horn between his eyes.

6 And he came to the ram that had two horns, which I had seen standing before the river, and ran unto him in the fury of his power.

7 And I saw him come close unto the ram, and he was moved with choler against him, and smote the ram, and brake his two horns: and there was no power in the ram to stand before him, but he cast him down to the ground, and stamped upon him: and there was none that could deliver the ram out of his hand.

8 Therefore the he goat waxed very great: and when he was strong, the great horn was broken; and for it came up four notable ones toward the four winds of heaven.

9 And out of one of them came forth a little horn, which waxed exceeding great, toward the south, and toward the east, and toward the pleasant land.

10 And it waxed great, even to the host of heaven; and it cast down some of the host and of the stars to the ground, and stamped upon them.

11 Yea, he magnified himself even to the prince of the host, and by him the daily sacrifice was taken away, and the place of the sanctuary was cast down.

12 And an host was given him against the daily sacrifice by reason of transgression, and it cast down the truth to the ground; and it practised, and prospered.

13 Then I heard one saint speaking, and another saint said unto that certain saint which spake, How long shall be the vision concerning the daily sacrifice, and the transgression of desolation, to give both the sanctuary and the host to be trodden under foot?

14 And he said unto me, Unto two thousand and three hundred days; then shall the sanctuary be cleansed.

15 And it came to pass, when I, even I Daniel, had seen the vision, and sought for the meaning, then, behold, there stood before me as the appearance of a man.

16 And I heard a man's voice between the banks of Ulai, which called, and said, Gabriel, make this man to understand the vision.

17 So he came near where I stood: and when he came, I was afraid, and fell upon my face: but he said unto me, Understand, O son of man: for at the time of the end shall be the vision.

18 Now as he was speaking with me, I was in a deep sleep on my face toward the ground: but he touched me, and set me upright.

19 And he said, Behold, I will make thee know what shall be in the last end of the indignation: for at the time appointed the end shall be.

20 The ram which thou sawest having two horns are the kings of Media and Persia.

21 And the rough goat is the king of Grecia: and the great horn that is between his eyes is the first king.

22 Now that being broken, whereas four stood up for it, four kingdoms shall stand up out of the nation, but not in his power.

23 And in the latter time of their kingdom, when the transgressors are come to the full, a king of fierce countenance, and understanding dark sentences, shall stand up.

24 And his power shall be mighty, but not by his own power: and he shall destroy wonderfully, and shall prosper, and practise, and shall destroy the mighty and the holy people.

25 And through his policy also he shall cause craft to prosper in his hand; and he shall magnify himself in his heart, and by peace shall destroy many: he shall also stand up against the Prince of princes; but he shall be broken without hand.

26 And the vision of the evening and the morning which was told is true: wherefore shut thou up the vision; for it shall be for many days.

27 And I Daniel fainted, and was sick certain days; afterward I rose up, and did the king's business; and I was astonished at the vision, but none understood it.

Daniel 9

1 In the first year of Darius the son of Ahasuerus, of the seed of the Medes, which was made king over the realm of the Chaldeans;

2In the first year of his reign I Daniel understood by books the number of the years, whereof the word of the LORD came to Jeremiah the prophet, that he would accomplish seventy years in the desolations of Jerusalem.

3And I set my face unto the Lord God, to seek by prayer and supplications, with fasting, and sackcloth, and ashes:

4 And I prayed unto the LORD my God, and made my confession, and said, O Lord, the great and dreadful God, keeping the covenant and mercy to them that love him, and to them that keep his commandments;

5 We have sinned, and have committed iniquity, and have done wickedly, and have rebelled, even by departing from thy precepts and from thy judgments:

6 Neither have we hearkened unto thy servants the prophets, which spake in thy name to our kings, our princes, and our fathers, and to all the people of the land.

7 O LORD, righteousness belongeth unto thee, but unto us confusion of faces, as at this day; to the men of Judah, and to the inhabitants of Jerusalem, and unto all Israel, that are near, and that are far off, through all the countries whither thou hast driven them, because of their trespass that they have trespassed against thee.

8 O Lord, to us belongeth confusion of face, to our kings, to our princes, and to our fathers, because we have sinned against thee.

9 To the Lord our God belong mercies and forgivenesses, though we have rebelled against him;

10 Neither have we obeyed the voice of the LORD our God, to walk in his laws, which he set before us by his servants the prophets.

11 Yea, all Israel have transgressed thy law, even by departing, that they might not obey thy voice; therefore the curse is poured upon us, and the oath that is written in the law of Moses the servant of God, because we have sinned against him.

12 And he hath confirmed his words, which he spake against us, and against our judges that judged us, by bringing upon us a great evil: for under the whole heaven hath not been done as hath been done upon Jerusalem.

13 As it is written in the law of Moses, all this evil is come upon us: yet made we not our prayer before the LORD our God, that we might turn from our iniquities, and understand thy truth.

14 Therefore hath the LORD watched upon the evil, and brought it upon us: for the LORD our God is righteous in all his works which he doeth: for we obeyed not his voice.

15 And now, O Lord our God, that hast brought thy people forth out of the land of Egypt with a mighty hand, and hast gotten thee renown, as at this day; we have sinned, we have done wickedly.

16 O LORD, according to all thy righteousness, I beseech thee, let thine anger and thy fury be turned away from thy city Jerusalem, thy holy mountain: because for our sins, and for the iniquities of our fathers, Jerusalem and thy people are become a reproach to all that are about us.

17 Now therefore, O our God, hear the prayer of thy servant, and his supplications, and cause thy face to shine upon thy sanctuary that is desolate, for the Lord's sake.

18 O my God, incline thine ear, and hear; open thine eyes, and behold our desolations, and the city which is called by thy name: for we do not present our supplications before thee for our righteousnesses, but for thy great mercies.

19 O Lord, hear; O Lord, forgive; O Lord, hearken and do; defer not, for thine own sake, O my God: for thy city and thy people are called by thy name.

20 And whiles I was speaking, and praying, and confessing my sin and the sin of my people Israel, and presenting my supplication before the LORD my God for the holy mountain of my God;

21 Yea, whiles I was speaking in prayer, even the man Gabriel, whom I had seen in the vision at the beginning, being caused to fly swiftly, touched me about the time of the evening oblation.

22 And he informed me, and talked with me, and said, O Daniel, I am now come forth to give thee skill and understanding.

23 At the beginning of thy supplications the commandment came forth, and I am come to shew thee; for thou art greatly beloved: therefore understand the matter, and consider the vision.

24 Seventy weeks are determined upon thy people and upon thy holy city, to finish the transgression, and to make an end of sins, and to make reconciliation for iniquity, and to bring in everlasting righteousness, and to seal up the vision and prophecy, and to anoint the most Holy.

25 Know therefore and understand, that from the going forth of the commandment to restore and to build Jerusalem unto the Messiah the Prince shall be seven weeks, and threescore and two weeks: the street shall be built again, and the wall, even in troublous times.

26 And after threescore and two weeks shall Messiah be cut off, but not for himself: and the people of the prince that shall come shall destroy the city and the sanctuary; and the end thereof shall be with a flood, and unto the end of the war desolations are determined.

27 And he shall confirm the covenant with many for one week: and in the midst of the week he shall cause the sacrifice and the oblation to cease, and for the overspreading of abominations he shall make it desolate, even until the consummation, and that determined shall be poured upon the desolate.

Daniel 10

1 In the third year of Cyrus king of Persia a thing was revealed unto Daniel, whose name was called Belteshazzar; and the

thing was true, but the time appointed was long: and he understood the thing, and had understanding of the vision.

2 In those days I Daniel was mourning three full weeks.

3 I ate no pleasant bread, neither came flesh nor wine in my mouth, neither did I anoint myself at all, till three whole weeks were fulfilled.

4 And in the four and twentieth day of the first month, as I was by the side of the great river, which is Hiddekel;

5 Then I lifted up mine eyes, and looked, and behold a certain man clothed in linen, whose loins were girded with fine gold of Uphaz:

6 His body also was like the beryl, and his face as the appearance of lightning, and his eyes as lamps of fire, and his arms and his feet like in colour to polished brass, and the voice of his words like the voice of a multitude.

7 And I Daniel alone saw the vision: for the men that were with me saw not the vision; but a great quaking fell upon them, so that they fled to hide themselves.

8 Therefore I was left alone, and saw this great vision, and there remained no strength in me: for my comeliness was turned in me into corruption, and I retained no strength.

9 Yet heard I the voice of his words: and when I heard the voice of his words, then was I in a deep sleep on my face, and my face toward the ground.

10 And, behold, an hand touched me, which set me upon my knees and upon the palms of my hands.

11 And he said unto me, O Daniel, a man greatly beloved, understand the words that I speak unto thee, and stand upright: for unto thee am I now sent. And when he had spoken this word unto me, I stood trembling.

12 Then said he unto me, Fear not, Daniel: for from the first day that thou didst set thine heart to understand, and to chasten thyself before thy God, thy words were heard, and I am come for thy words.

13 But the prince of the kingdom of Persia withstood me one and twenty days: but, lo, Michael, one of the chief princes, came to help me; and I remained there with the kings of Persia.

14 Now I am come to make thee understand what shall befall thy people in the latter days: for yet the vision is for many days.

15 And when he had spoken such words unto me, I set my face toward the ground, and I became dumb.

16 And, behold, one like the similitude of the sons of men touched my lips: then I opened my mouth, and spake, and said unto him that stood before me, O my lord, by the vision my sorrows are turned upon me, and I have retained no strength.

17 For how can the servant of this my lord talk with this my lord? for as for me, straightway there remained no strength in me, neither is there breath left in me.

18 Then there came again and touched me one like the appearance of a man, and he strengthened me,

19 And said, O man greatly beloved, fear not: peace be unto thee, be strong, yea, be strong. And when he had spoken unto me, I was strengthened, and said, Let my lord speak; for thou hast strengthened me.

20 Then said he, Knowest thou wherefore I come unto thee? and now will I return to fight with the prince of Persia: and when I am gone forth, lo, the prince of Grecia shall come.

21 But I will shew thee that which is noted in the scripture of truth: and there is none that holdeth with me in these things, but Michael your prince.

Daniel 11

1 Also I in the first year of Darius the Mede, even I, stood to confirm and to strengthen him.

2 And now will I shew thee the truth. Behold, there shall stand up yet three kings in Persia; and the fourth shall be far richer than they all: and by his strength through his riches he shall stir up all against the realm of Grecia.

3And a mighty king shall stand up, that shall rule with great dominion, and do according to his will.

4 And when he shall stand up, his kingdom shall be broken, and shall be divided toward the four winds of heaven; and not to his posterity, nor according to his dominion which he ruled: for his kingdom shall be plucked up, even for others beside those.

5 And the king of the south shall be strong, and one of his princes; and he shall be strong above him, and have dominion; his dominion shall be a great dominion.

6 And in the end of years they shall join themselves together; for the king's daughter of the south shall come to the king of the north to make an agreement: but she shall not retain the power of the arm; neither shall he stand, nor his arm: but she shall be given up, and they that brought her, and he that begat her, and he that strengthened her in these times.

7 But out of a branch of her roots shall one stand up in his estate, which shall come with an army, and shall enter into the fortress of the king of the north, and shall deal against them, and shall prevail:

8 And shall also carry captives into Egypt their gods, with their princes, and with their precious vessels of silver and of gold; and he shall continue more years than the king of the north.

9 So the king of the south shall come into his kingdom, and shall return into his own land.

10 But his sons shall be stirred up, and shall assemble a multitude of great forces: and one shall certainly come, and overflow, and pass through: then shall he return, and be stirred up, even to his fortress.

11 And the king of the south shall be moved with choler, and shall come forth and fight with him, even with the king of the north: and he shall set forth a great multitude; but the multitude shall be given into his hand.

12 And when he hath taken away the multitude, his heart shall be lifted up; and he shall cast down many ten thousands: but he shall not be strengthened by it.

13 For the king of the north shall return, and shall set forth a multitude greater than the former, and shall certainly come after certain years with a great army and with much riches.

14 And in those times there shall many stand up against the king of the south: also the robbers of thy people shall exalt themselves to establish the vision; but they shall fall.

15 So the king of the north shall come, and cast up a mount, and take the most fenced cities: and the arms of the south shall not withstand, neither his chosen people, neither shall there be any strength to withstand.

16 But he that cometh against him shall do according to his own will, and none shall stand before him: and he shall stand in the glorious land, which by his hand shall be consumed.

17 He shall also set his face to enter with the strength of his whole kingdom, and upright ones with him; thus shall he do: and he shall give him the daughter of women, corrupting her: but she shall not stand on his side, neither be for him.

18 After this shall he turn his face unto the isles, and shall take many: but a prince for his own behalf shall cause the reproach offered by him to cease; without his own reproach he shall cause it to turn upon him.

19 Then he shall turn his face toward the fort of his own land: but he shall stumble and fall, and not be found.

20 Then shall stand up in his estate a raiser of taxes in the glory of the kingdom: but within few days he shall be destroyed, neither in anger, nor in battle.

21 And in his estate shall stand up a vile person, to whom they shall not give the honour of the kingdom: but he shall come in peaceably, and obtain the kingdom by flatteries.

22 And with the arms of a flood shall they be overflown from before him, and shall be broken; yea, also the prince of the covenant.

23 And after the league made with him he shall work deceitfully: for he shall come up, and shall become strong with a small people.

24 He shall enter peaceably even upon the fattest places of the province; and he shall do that which his fathers have not done, nor his fathers' fathers; he shall scatter among them the prey, and spoil, and riches: yea, and he shall forecast his devices against the strong holds, even for a time.

25 And he shall stir up his power and his courage against the king of the south with a great army; and the king of the south shall be stirred up to battle with a very great and mighty army; but he shall not stand: for they shall forecast devices against him.

26 Yea, they that feed of the portion of his meat shall destroy him, and his army shall overflow: and many shall fall down slain.

27 And both of these kings' hearts shall be to do mischief, and they shall speak lies at one table; but it shall not prosper: for yet the end shall be at the time appointed.

28 Then shall he return into his land with great riches; and his heart shall be against the holy covenant; and he shall do exploits, and return to his own land.

29 At the time appointed he shall return, and come toward the south; but it shall not be as the former, or as the latter.

30 For the ships of Chittim shall come against him: therefore he shall be grieved, and return, and have indignation against the holy covenant: so shall he do; he shall even return, and have intelligence with them that forsake the holy covenant.

31 And arms shall stand on his part, and they shall pollute the sanctuary of strength, and shall take away the daily sacrifice, and they shall place the abomination that maketh desolate.

32 And such as do wickedly against the covenant shall he corrupt by flatteries: but the people that do know their God shall be strong, and do exploits.

33 And they that understand among the people shall instruct many: yet they shall fall by the sword, and by flame, by captivity, and by spoil, many days.

34 Now when they shall fall, they shall be holpen with a little help: but many shall cleave to them with flatteries.

35 And some of them of understanding shall fall, to try them, and to purge, and to make them white, even to the time of the end: because it is yet for a time appointed.

36 And the king shall do according to his will; and he shall exalt himself, and magnify himself above every god, and shall speak marvellous things against the God of gods, and shall prosper till the indignation be accomplished: for that that is determined shall be done.

37 Neither shall he regard the God of his fathers, nor the desire of women, nor regard any god: for he shall magnify himself above all.

38 But in his estate shall he honour the God of forces: and a god whom his fathers knew not shall he honour with gold, and silver, and with precious stones, and pleasant things.

39 Thus shall he do in the most strong holds with a strange god, whom he shall acknowledge and increase with glory: and he shall cause them to rule over many, and shall divide the land for gain.

40 And at the time of the end shall the king of the south push at him: and the king of the north shall come against him like

a whirlwind, with chariots, and with horsemen, and with many ships; and he shall enter into the countries, and shall overflow and pass over.

41 He shall enter also into the glorious land, and many countries shall be overthrown: but these shall escape out of his hand, even Edom, and Moab, and the chief of the children of Ammon.

42 He shall stretch forth his hand also upon the countries: and the land of Egypt shall not escape.

43 But he shall have power over the treasures of gold and of silver, and over all the precious things of Egypt: and the Libyans and the Ethiopians shall be at his steps.

44 But tidings out of the east and out of the north shall trouble him: therefore he shall go forth with great fury to destroy, and utterly to make away many.

45 And he shall plant the tabernacles of his palace between the seas in the glorious holy mountain; yet he shall come to his end, and none shall help him.

Daniel 12

1 And at that time shall Michael stand up, the great prince which standeth for the children of thy people: and there shall be a time of trouble, such as never was since there was a nation

even to that same time: and at that time thy people shall be delivered, every one that shall be found written in the book.

2 And many of them that sleep in the dust of the earth shall awake, some to everlasting life, and some to shame and everlasting contempt.

3 And they that be wise shall shine as the brightness of the firmament; and they that turn many to righteousness as the stars for ever and ever.

4 But thou, O Daniel, shut up the words, and seal the book, even to the time of the end: many shall run to and fro, and knowledge shall be increased.

5 Then I Daniel looked, and, behold, there stood other two, the one on this side of the bank of the river, and the other on that side of the bank of the river.

6 And one said to the man clothed in linen, which was upon the waters of the river, How long shall it be to the end of these wonders?

7 And I heard the man clothed in linen, which was upon the waters of the river, when he held up his right hand and his left hand unto heaven, and sware by him that liveth for ever that it shall be for a time, times, and an half; and when he shall

have accomplished to scatter the power of the holy people, all these things shall be finished.

8 And I heard, but I understood not: then said I, O my Lord, what shall be the end of these things?

9 And he said, Go thy way, Daniel: for the words are closed up and sealed till the time of the end.

10 Many shall be purified, and made white, and tried; but the wicked shall do wickedly: and none of the wicked shall understand; but the wise shall understand.

11 And from the time that the daily sacrifice shall be taken away, and the abomination that maketh desolate set up, there shall be a thousand two hundred and ninety days.

12 Blessed is he that waiteth, and cometh to the thousand three hundred and five and thirty days.

13 But go thou thy way till the end be: for thou shalt rest, and stand in thy lot at the end of the days.

In the book of Daniel 12:4. **But thou, O Daniel, shut up the words, and seal the book, even to the time of the end: many shall run to and fro, and knowledge shall be increased.**
Will another great leader be destroyed are will another be born. It's not in our understanding what shell be bough

about. Whether it's the beginning of the end of time; it's not in our power to know. Man has tried to predict the end of days for decades.

For the Holy Bible states that no man knows the time or day that the LORD will come. But He gives clues to the beginning of sorrow. I say, all we can do is watch and pray.

When we resist our faith we suffer. When we come to terms in the faith, we'll be at peace.

It may always be a mystery to some, why these great people past on. I say, God's hand has its power. So let's just remember what they lived For. These were some many great personality that perished.

We can't live a truly and committed life without taking a stand.

"In today's news, September 20, 2001, U.S. President George W. Bush, before a joint session of Congress, declares war on international terrorism. This is the U.S. press signing out."

President Bush widely suspects Al-Qaeda forces and other terror cells of possessing nuclear weapons. Nadia decides she needs a breath of fresh-air after the bad news on terrorism she visits the festival.

Nadia is walking around the festival. She's looking for her roommate Reshema. Terser recognizes Nadia walking in the opposite direction.

"Is that Nadia? It is Nadia?" Say's Terser.

"Hay, Nadia. We're over here." Say's Reshema.

Nadia locates her friends as she walks in their direction.

"Hi, how is everyone?" Say's Nadia.

"What a surprise! What made you change your mind?" Say's Reshema.

"It's just a last minute decision. The TV news upset me."

"I'm glad you made it. I was beginning to think schoolwork was the only thing you took serious in life." Say's Terser.

"My education is my life. This is why I'm here."

"I can respect that. I see you have your priorities in order. Nevertheless, you know the old saying. All work and no play make a dull man."

"Are you calling me dull?"

"No. I'm not saying that. I just want to make sure you don't become bored."

"Well, guys, we're going in the opposite direction. Have fun. Say's Ausan.

Ausan and Reshema walk away and Terser and Nadia stands alone and talk.

"So tell me. What does a serious lady as yourself enjoy doing in your spare time?"

"Let's see. I like to play chess, and I like reading action adventure novels and Biblical stories." Reading in your spare time sounds like homework.

Playing chess, sounds like you were on the debate team in high school.

"Well, reading in my spare time is not like homework. When you open your mind freely with no obligation and experience your spirit taking you to new places, it's magical. Nevertheless, I was, on the high school debate team."

"With all the reading you must have gained a strong imagination. So tell me. How would you imagination the perfect romantic date?"

"Well, I imagine long walks in the moonlight with a clear sky so I can see the stars so bright. As the night turns to the break of dawn, I like the sunrise on a beach in the early morn."

"Woo. That's interesting. You see the sky is not so clear on tonight. There's no moon and no stars, and we're too far from away from an early morning sunrise. Well, what would you say to a stroll down the boardwalk and a nice cool snowball and fireworks?"

"Fireworks you say."

Terser pulls from his pocket a box of sparklers. He stops at the snowball stand and purchases two snowballs. He pulls out one sparkler.

"Here. Take this."

He pulls out a liter and ignites the sparkler.

"Oh, no! Here take it. Take it. Say's Nadia

"Are you afraid of a few sparkles?"

She runs down the boardwalk laughing. Terser run behind her until the sparkler burns out. He catches her and grabs her hand.

Ok. It's out. It's out.

They stop and face one another and laugh. The festival's fireworks go off deep into the sky. He wholes her close.

'Happy New Year's.'

Terser and Nadia become close for the next five years. They complete their college education as they prepare for their day of graduation.

Nadia and Reshema prepare in the dorm room for the day of graduation.

"I will miss you." Say's Reshema.

"I will miss you also."

They hug as Nadia begins to cry and she breaks away and runs to the restroom.

"Nadia are you ok?"

"Yes. Oh, Reshema. Oh, Reshema.

She vomits in the bathroom.

"What? Tell me. Did Terser upset you?"

"No Reshema. I'm pregnant."

"Oh, my. Well, congratulations. Does he know?"

"No."

"You must tell him."

"I know. I will tell him tonight."

CHAPTER 9

On the evening the students are gathering in the auditorium. Terser walks over to Nadia and hugs her. "Hi, Nadia. I haven't seen you all day. Congratulations, we finally made it. What's the problem? You look unhappy."

"I need to talk to you. It's very important."

The students are called to the line to start the ceremony.

"Ok. They're calling us. Let's talk later."

Terser and Nadia walk to their seating area. The ceremony begins. After the ceremony they meet in the lobby.

"Was there something important you had to tell me?" Say's Terser.

"Yes."

Nadia becomes overheated and passes out in Terser arms.

"Nadia, Nadia. Are you ok? Some help. We need help."

Nadia is taken for help. After Nadia's test result.

"How long have you known?"

"For three weeks."

"Well, you were a little dehydrated and I have some additional information to tell you."

"What is it?"

"You're having twins."

"Are you sure?"

"I'm positive. Also you have some friends outside waiting to see you. Would you like to see visitors"

"Yes."

The assistant walks to the visitor lobby and informs Terser and Reshema that Nadia would like to see them.

"Hi, I was worried." Say's Terser.

"I'm ok. Reshema, I need to talk to Terser. Give us a minute."

"Ok. I'll be in the lobby. Take your time."

A special news bulletin flashes across the TV screen. Nadia pauses to see the news as the media make clear in their exhaustive investigation into this issue, the degradation of civilians by U.S. troops has become commonplace in Iraq.

Another news bulletin flashes across the T.V.

"The overlooked players in the torture scandal are the medical personnel who supervise—and often participate in —an act of torture. Military medical professionals' conscience should tell them to take an ethical stand. Though they're not the usual suspects, they should be investigated as well. This is Jonathan reporting from The Nation."

"In the news, today- The Iraqi government said it will file criminal charges against employees of security firm Blackwater USA. The Iraqi government claims the private contractors, who were guarding a U.S. diplomatic convoy, as many as 20 civilians was lost. Iraqi officials, who claim the shooting was unprovoked, dispute Blackwater's claim that the guards were responding to an unknown approach of a vehicle and said on Saturday they had a video tape showing the Blackwater guards opened fire without provocation. This is the Nation's News."

"The conditions in the world are not getting any better. We're seeing more of the signs of the end of time. Come over and sit. I've tried to tell you something all day." Say's Nadia.

"What is it?"

"We'll be ok. Will you marry me?

"There's more. It's twins." Say's Nadia.

"Wahoo, twins. Don't worry we'll be ok. I'll ask you again. Will you marry me?"

"It's not necessary that you do this."

"I know. But I love you. Will you say yes?"

"Yes. I also love you."

Terser and Nadia gets married, and Terser reveals to Nadia that he's received a job offer with the Pakistani government.

"I've received a job offer in with the Pakistani government. I'm going to the interview, and I will be back shortly."

Terser returns to Pakistan as he visits his family. "Welcome home, my son. I have waited for this moment for some time now. You can now join the Taliban.

"Wait. I must tell you. My views of the Taliban have changed. I know longer believe in a religion of violence for spiritual gain."

"That's blasphemy. Through the Koran we have a right."

"Wait,. I have a family now. I will go and get them. You will see more of who I am now."

Terser return and sits in the waiting room as Nadia prepares for delivery.

"Hi. How are you?"

"I'm well." Say's Nadia.

"You look great. The boys are healthy. You should rest, and we will talk later."

Terser sits in the chair at Nadia's bedside. She sleeps for a while and awakens.

"How do you feel? I spoke to my family recently at home. He was very upset with me. He didn't understand the change of my spiritual views. I told him about you."

"Don't worry. He may need some time to adjust." Say's Nadia.

"I don't know. You just don't know him. I hope he will understand once he see my sons."

"You should take one of the boys now to see him and take the other later. Once I'm released, you can take me to visit your family."

"Family means everything to him. I think this is a good idea. This is his phone number. If you need me call."

After a few days Terser take one of the boys and visits in Pakistan.

"Hello, this is my son. This is your grandson. Look he has your eyes."

Terser's are very happy to see their grandson.

"Take me to the market. I will cook and we will celebrate."

Terser and one parent are on their way to the market. Terser slowly approaches a barricade of U.S. military. The soldiers are spooked by gunfire in the background. They open fire on the vehicle of Terser.

"No. No. What have we done? She says.

Terser says his last words.

A special news bulletin appears across the TV screen. A close up is shown of Terser. He is pulled from the car.

"One day in January 2005, two people was driving down the road in Mosul, Iraq, when without realizing it they passed through a makeshift U.S. military checkpoint. The checkpoint, said a sergeant who came upon the scene, was "very poorly marked." Yet, he said, the soldiers "got spooked" and opened fire."

"No! It can't be. No Terser. Please no."

Nadia's is consoles. Nadia picks up the phone and she searches for the number to Terser's home. She calls for Terser.

"Yes."

"Tell me it's not so."

"Yes. He's no longer with us."

"My God! What about my Little T"?"

"He is well."

"I must come and get him.

"There's no need. You took my son away from me when you turned him away from his God. Now I will take your son, and I will raise him to be the son I once had. A son the Radicals can be proud of."

"No. You can't. You can't take my son."

1st Seal White Horse conquering Rev.6-1,2

The False Profit talk's peace between Pakistan and Israel. The ten most powerful Nation in the world gather together view. The President confirms a 7 year covenant on the signing of the Middle-East Peace treaty.

False Profit

"This is a day of peace and future progress." Jerusalem-The groundbreaking on the Jerusalem Temple is introduced by the New President.

False Profit

"We will now make an image of a new world order leader and we shell make peace that will emphasize full rights of religious group and minorities."

In the Middle East the deluding influence sent by God upon unbeliever will be the start of the mark of the beast. It's now present, 666.

Dr. Yu. In my sleep for day after the event an influence of the time 3:33 was a puzzling repartition each morning of awaking at this time of 3:33from the time I starting writing the book. This time begin to draw my attention also during each day's activity. I also ask myself what does this mean. It wasn't until recently it came to me in my visions of a formula. It incorporated the three numbers with three calculations, of the year 2020 as seen in my earlier writing. It was also with the number of the beast 666.

The number is describe is biblical scripture as the number of a man. Can this number be the birth number of a man. Who knows! As I made my first dream calculation, it gave me a date I foresaw. 7/1/2013.

6 6 6

06.06.2060

2020

3:33
_____

7113

7/1/2013

I researched this date, as I made a Internet web search. Question? What World event accrued on 7/1/2013 that changed the course of world history? And it gave me the following headlines.

This week in history

Egypt
July 1, 2013

Citizens staged huge protest
Across Egypt calling for the resignation
Of President Morsi in the largest
Demonstration since the revolution
In 2011. Protesters were upset that
Morsi had not fixed the security
problems in the country.

The elimination of Christian was the main reasons that lead to this protest that called for the resignation of President Morsi in the largest demonstration since the revolution in 2011. The formula present here is within my dream prophecy as I envision that which is relevant to future date in time. These dates are relative dates to the destruction of Christians or people of Christ and other biblical prophecies in the future.

As I made my remaining Dream calculation, it gave me the dates. 1/3/2060, and or 1/13/2060, 5/6/2060, 5/9/2060 and 5/9/2060 and don't forget the Year-2020. These dates may play a significant role and parallel to the 7/1/2013 event in the change of history as we know it.

Whatever future events appear within these calculations I, want to make sure I am drawn to the fullness of the faith. Science will never triumph over religion. God has calculated all his mysterious just as the number of "every hair on a man's head is numbered." If this prove nothing more, then to justify that God has his hand in many things of Increased Knowledge.

In the end-times, "Knowledge Increased" age will unlock secretes and open understanding to prophecy. In the beginning of the New Age area of "Increase Knowledge" a very strategic form of New-age- technology known as satellite Network TV appeared. This technology will revolve and have a great impact revealing biblical history and prophecy in the future. We will see technology in the government as monitoring individuals through government secret serves satellites. This means viewing people through Televisions, and their Cell phones. (T.V. @ Cell Video Monitoring)

This technology will solidify the scriptures as it will take part in future as we see one of the return of the Lord and Savior Christ. Revelation 1:7 tells us "Behold, He cometh with a cloud, and **every eye shall see him**, and they also witch pierced him: and all kindred's of the earth shell wail because of him. This technology will take part in Christ appearance as the church of the earlier age couldn't see the full concept in this vision, as New Age technology has given us more clarity today.

There are so many prophecies in place today in the twenty century (2014), as we see more of the beginning of one world changing events. The coming will not be far away, as no man knows the time that the Lord shall come, but God will show many signs.

"But thou, O Daniel, shut up the words, and seal the book, even to the time of the end: many shell run to and fro, and knowledge shell be increase."
Daniel 12: 4

And it was said by another writer of today: "A portion of the book of Daniel was not going to be understood "until the time of the end. At the time of the end, many would run to and fro through the scriptures, comparing text with text, and understand these prophecies.

The bible also predicts a time when it will be to late to search the scriptures, "Behold, the days come, said the Lord GOD, that I will send a famine in the land, not a famine of bread,, nor a thirst of water, but a hearing of the word of the LORD. And they shell wonder from sea to sea, and from north to the east, they shall run to and fro to seek the word of the LORD, and not find it. In that day shell virgins and young men faint for thirst. "Amos 8:11-13

It is reality that the vast majority of the word will be without God and with hope when Christ returns, the bible also says that many people will understand, prepare, and be ready. Many shell be purified, and made white, and tried; but the wickedly shell be wickedly: and none of the wicked shell understand; but the wise shell understand. Daniel:12:10

The primary application of "knowledge increased" is a reference to people understanding the prophecies of the book of Daniel, however, many Bible scholars believe that this prophecy also applies to an increasing knowledge of science, medicine, travel, and technology.

We are living in "The Information Age" making this sign seem even more obvious. Even the most skeptical mind must admit that knowledge is exploding in all directions. It is said that 80% percent of the world total knowledge has been brought forth in the last decade and that 90% percent of all the scientists who have ever lived are alive today.

The President of the United States visits Jerusalem to talk of peace between Pakistan and Israel. The President proposes a plan to strengthen the wall across the border dividing the nation of Jerusalem.

'This is the one last dream I had after receiving Nadia story in on that day as we sat in a restaurant. Two days later I had a future dream that extended her story.'

CHAPTER 10

Approximately, fifty years later Nadia and her second son sit as they watch the morning news. The camera shows the headshots of the Taliban radical's armed forces. The headshot of the captain appears. Nadia recognizes the captain to be her long lost son. He is the split image of her twin. Her son walks close to the TV in shock.

"It's my son. I prayed the day I would see him again."

"He's your son? He's a tyrant. He looks just like me. I don't understand."

Nadia reaches for a box behind a dresser. She pulls a book open to get a photo.

"Sit here. Let us talk. This is a photo of me, and your twin"

"He's my twin?"

"Yes. I never talk about it. I've tried to suppress it because it's too painful for me. I lost him. The Capitan resented the fact that I was the influence of Tarser turning away from the radicals. The Capitan was set to be the next leader. So he pledged to make me pay by taking my son."

The wall is now built between Pakistan and Israel.

The boarder is highly protected on both sides. Across the border in Pakistan, the captain Nadia's long lost son plans to build a tunnel from one end of the border across the other.

"From inside this building location, we will build a tunnel from this end to the inside of Israel borders. We have an inside man who will help accomplish our goal. Say's the Captain."

Nadia's son is home in bed. He pulls out the photo of the family given to him. He's thinking about of traveling to Pakistan to meet his twin and connect him to his family.

"I've been thinking for some time now. I need to take a trip."

"Where are you going?"

"I'm going to Pakistan to see him"

"No. It's dangerous. How would you get across the border?"

"I have a friend who can help. This is something I must do."

Nadia son packs a bag. He prepares to meet a friend to help cross the border. Nadia sits as she views the television and a special news bulletin flash across the screen.

"In the news today and United States economies hit an all-time low. This is the lowest ever seen in the history of these nations. The stock market has plummeted to and all-time low as natural disasters plague the nations like never before. Social Security is no longer in existence. The triad market is cut off to the American nation, and crude oil is no longer shipped to this country. The influence is the result of new radical leader of the nation of Israel. All nations have declared war on Israel."

"In today's news, a million people are missing in earthquakes during 20th century, and scientists acknowledge that the 21st century might see 10 times as many incidents, with a million lost in a single blow."

"Today in the news, Earthquake experts said the Eastern Seaboard is in more danger then ever. Earthquakes on the east coast will be most dangerous because they are abysmally unprepared, with building standards far less stringent then California, which is earthquake country. Volcano's and volcano eruption ash can cover over 90% of America."

"In world the News today. A plague of epidemics is beginning to worry public health officials all around the world. AIDS is only the most of these "new" diseases- the Ebola virus, mad cow disease, swine flue and many others scarcely heard of just ten years ago are now worrying public health experts worldwide Malaria is reemerging as super, drug-resistant diseases that ignore penicillin and other medications that were formerly used to combat them."

On one night Nadia's son meets his friend at the truck yard to help him cross the border.

"We have to be careful if we're going to do this. Once a month I transport a shipment across the border. I will put you in one of the containers. They never check all containers. They normally check for radiation and explosives with hi-technical devices. You have to find a way back without my help. I'll never know when we'll go back over the border."

Nadia's son successfully crosses the border with no interference. He is dropped off in a secured location with a map.

In the future, Worldwide famine engenders vicious competition and strife among the nations over food. Fish in the sea die at a rapid rate, and those that are alive are affected by the red tide disease. Food market stores are closing because of a high shortage of food. Theft increases throughout the nation and among the people.

WAR- 2nd Seal RED HORSE OF WAR Rev.6-3,4

Rev.6:3-And when he had open the Second seal, I heard the second beast say, Come and see. Rev. 6:4-And there went out another horse that was red: And power was given to him that sat thereon to take peace from the earth and that they should destroy one another: and there was given to him a great sword.

Within the destruction of land by atomic war the people could not burry their people. Examiners shell come from afar in protective gear to collect their bodies. All of a sudden, the sky unfolded as the clouds opened. The impact was so powerful it shakes the earth off its axis. In a wink of an eye, this war comes to a halt. Ships come from afar with people covered in bio-chemical-protected uniforms from head to toe as they exited the ships and examined the scene to bury the lost.

Nadia's lost son the captain stands as he supports the speech and influence of a false religious leader. He sits high on a platform before both the Pakistan and Israel nation. News leaders from across the nations are present to view the speech and the events.

5th Seal ANTICHRIST- BROUGHT BACK TO LIFE. (White Horse conquering Rev.6-1,2)

As the Antichrist is bought back to life in a stunning event the false religious leader will sit aside the end-time beast. Perhaps as well, the end-time beast maybe one who will resurface out of hiding after the attempt of his destruction. But yet power destruction, The End-Time Beast, shell appear and deceive with miracles. The End-Time beast will make a speech to the presenting a New World Order.

"Come my people and witness the power of your Lord. From this day forward every nation shall serve and no one will eat unless they buy from me."

The false religious leader sits astride the end-time "Beast" which is the king from the north. The false prophet then gives the leaders a sign to secretly ignite a satellite laser from the sky.

He lifts up his hands and cause fire to come down from the sky. He persuades the nation in thinking he has a powerful gift.

A Decree is made by the false prophet that all people make a Image of the Antichrist.

The people are now ordered to go to the government offices in various locations and receive individual personal identification cards. This card contain personal information of each individual, personal picture ID number, religious sect, and the government number 666 over the head of the card and in many cases in the hand. Many Christians and other target group, will follow the control, of the Beast and in their hand implanted a tracking device of a microchip. He then provokes and confronts two ready–made enemies. One would be U.S.A and the other Russia. All other nations will take part as the anti-Christ increase terrorism and have the power of oil, and all other commodities which will be denied to its adversaries, and the Holly War begins.

Then the decline and collapse of the English-speaking nation struck by their enemies reveals that indescribably terrifying time in the entire history of the planet that is called The Great Tribulation.

3^{ed} Trumpet Rev. 8:10-11

A stair fall and the name of the star is called wormwood, and a third of the waters become wormwood. Many of the people die from the waters, because they had been made bitter. Rev. 8:10-111/3 of the rivers and streams are poisoned.

During this time, a worldwide famine engenders vicious competition and strife among the nations over food. Fish in the sea dies at a rapid rate, and the red tide disease affects those that are alive. Food market stores are closing because of a high shortage of food. Theft increases throughout the nation and among the people.

One of our most challenging wars in the medical field today is against influential various misdirecting the full various from engaging it host. Therefore, a pre-injected strain which is an anti-various strain is injected into the host to fight out. It tells the various "where're already here.' Therefore, the various don't infect its own.

But there will come a time during the beginning of sorrow where different anti- bodies of strains will not resists the anti-various. Inflectional-Disease will destroy millions during these end-times.

3ed Seal BLACK HORSE OF FAMINE

5: And when he had open the third seal, I heard the beast say, Come and see. And I beheld, and lo a black horse; and he that sat on him had a pair of balance in his hand:

6: And I heard a voice say, A measure of wheat for a penny, and three measures of barley for a penny; and see they hurt not the oil and the wine.

Rev.6-5,6

"Bread for sale! Bread for sale! Get your bread for $20 a loaf. I have three pounds of flour, $20 for three pounds." Say's a local merchant.

"I need oil to cook the flour. Do you have oil or wine?" Say's a local buyer.

"There's no more oil in the whole state. Only bread and flour." Say's the merchant.

All of a sudden, the sky unfolded as the clouds opened. The impact was so powerful it shakes the earth off its axis. In a wink of an eye, this war comes to a halt. It comes to pass, after the smoke clears, that the meteorite was actually a Solar Satellite Laser. In this land the people cannot bury their, for there are only smoke and bones as far as the eye can see.

Ships come from afar with people covered in bio-chemical-protected uniforms from head to toe as they exited the ships and examined the scene to bury the lost.

WAR- 4th seal PALE HORSE Power given to the Anti- Christ Rev.6-7,(8 MAT:24:9

Rev. 6:7- And when he had open the forth seal, I heard the voice of the forth beast say, come and see.

Rev. 6:8- And I looked, and behold a pale horse: and his name that sat on him was death, and Hell followed with him. And power was given unto them over the forth part of the earth, and to kill with sword, and with hunger, and with death, and with the beast of the earth.

The people are now ordered to the government offices in various locations and receive their own person identification card representing the number 666.

This card contain personal information of each individual, personal picture ID number, religious sect, and the Anti-Christ incasing the New World Order. In their hand is implanted a microchip. Everyone must register by computer. World -Wide- Web. WWW 666" may be one form of the 666. (Revelation 13:16-18). The Greeks used letters as their numbers. Consequently, '666' in Greek could be written 'WWW'.

'Remember! Biblical scripture only describe this number 666 as the number of a man.' In heaven- God awards his people. REV.6:11

REV. 9 And when he had open the fifth seal I saw under the altar the souls of them that were slain for the world of God and for the testimony which they held.

SLAIN SOULS

And they Cried out with a loud voice 10-How long, O Loud, holy and true, dose thou not judge and avenge our blood on them that dwell on the earth?

Rev.6: 10-11
Rev.11-And white robes were given unto every one of them;

GOD

My children you should rest yet for a little season, until your fellow servants and your brethren that should be killed as you were, should be fulfilled.

The gospel of the kingdom is preached in the entire world for a witness unto all nations; this angers the king of the north, and the force of the king of the south is completely crushed by this power. The king of the north then comes down "like a whirlwind" and takes over the Middle East, including the Holy Land.

Then the great charismatic leader (Messiah) will gather together the forces of Islam in a final (holy war) against the corrupt nations, whose religion, and power represent a challenge to the Islamic faith as they see it. Their total mission is to destroy Israel.

Nadia's son is now in position as he poses as a cameraman to get close to the captain. He is under cover with a false beard and hairpiece. Nadia's son moves closer to the captain.

"Captain, I need to talk to you. It's very important." Say's Nadia's son.

The captain smiles for the camera and moves away. Nadia's son gets aggressive and approaches the captain and grabs him by the arm to get his attention. The captain's guards apprehend him and take him away. Nadia's son is held, as he demands to speak to the captain. They rip off his beard and hairpiece and interrogate him.

"Who are you? You are impersonating the captain." Say the lieutenant.

"I'm here to speak to the captain."

"Who do you work for and who gave you this face transformation?"

"I'm here alone. I work for no one and the captain must be informed of something important.

"I ask you again. Who are you?"

"Let me speak to the captain. I will explain it to him."

"No. Explain it to me. If not, we have our ways to make you talk."

Nadia's son is in solitary confinement. He is chained upright by both arms. The lieutenant enters the office to inform him of the imposter apprehended during the speech yesterday.

"Captain. The imposter we took on yesterday turns out to be a spy from Israel. They were attempting to infiltrate us by transforming him to look just like you. He came in undercover."

"You say he looks like me?"

"Yes. I think they were trying to replace you with him, but their plan failed. The stranger has information to tell you. Just because he's the image of you, he thinks he's someone you know"

The captain and the lieutenant begin to laugh.

"What a bold-face. He thinks this will free him? Take me to him. I'll get to the bottom of this."

The captain follows the lieutenant and two other guards to the cell."

"Wake him up." Say's the captain.

They pour water over his head. He lifts up his head. The captain looks him up and down from head to toe.

"They did a good job duplicating me. Who are you?"

"I'm someone you should know."

"What do you take me for? Now that you are captured this is the only excuse you can come up with? If I should know you, would I ask? I am running out of patience.

This is your last chance to prove yourself. Now, who are you?"

"Let me speak to you in private. Just give me a minute to prove myself."

The captain orders the lieutenant and the guards to step outside of the cell.

"Now, we're alone. So prove yourself.

"Reach into my back pocket. Get the photo."

The captain reaches into his back pocket and pulls out the photo.

"What's this? Why is he in you're photo?" Says the Captain.

"We are of the same blood. The two babies are the two of us. You were never informed just as I was. Let me tell you. After we were born, a visit was made with only you. They planned for me to come later. A trip was to the market and there was a bad accident. They were ambushed mistakenly as they entered a barricade by the U.S. army. He was lost on impact. There was misplaced blamed because of old anger. It was the turning away from Koran and renouncing Islam. So he kept you and promised to never let her see you again."

The captain puts the photo in his top pocket. The lieutenant looks around the corner as he becomes suspicious.

"If I find this to be false, I will take your life myself and with pleasure."

The captain turns and walks out of the cell.

The captain returns to his home where he grew up.

He makes a visit to his old home. He greets him with a hug.

"How are you? You look great."

"I'm so proud of you. I've seen you on TV. How is the fight against the enemy?"

"Listen. I need to ask a question. We captured a man we think is a spy. Take a look at this photo. Who is this in the photo? The spy says I should know him by this photo. Tell me, is it so?"

"My son, what have I done? Yes. It is so. It was too painful for me to accept. I lost my son, and I had nothing. You were all I had."

The captain hugs him and walks away. I must make this right."

At this time world war is at hand. Great armies from all nations are preparing for battle. Four great ships arise across the sun arisen from different nations in Jerusalem's off the coast of Gaza for the final desolation.

The captain is informed that western nations have crossed the oceans. The ships are firing artillery on land.

"All arms prepare to strike. All missiles strike west of the border." Say's the Captain.

"Captain, we must prepare to strike Israel as well." Say's the Lieutenant.

"Negative. You're ordered to handle the problem at hand."

"Something's not right. Say's the Lieutenant."

The lieutenant orders the guards to follow him. The captain is in route to the holding cell.

"Come, I must get you out of here. Hold on to me." "What's going on out there?"

"Pakistan is at war with the western nation. I have a way to get you across the border. We must act quietly."

"Why are you helping me?"

"This is what I must do. We must go. I know the way out."

The captain leads him to the secret tunnel that runs between both borders.

"How much further is the tunnel?"

"Just over there, in that building. In the right hand corner is a hatch that leads to the other side of the border."

The lieutenant and the guards locate the captain escorting and running towards the warehouse.

"Stop Captain. What are you doing? He's the enemy." Say's the Lieutenant.

"I know him." Say's the Captain.

"You can't do this. This is treason. I'm warning you stop or I will fire."

The captain stops and turns in front and shields the escorting man. He draws his weapon. The Captain is shot in the chest as he falls. The captain lies helpless as he is comforted. No. No.

All of a sudden, a missile is fired in the area of the Lieutenant and his guards. They are destroyed, as Nadia's son is safe on the ground with the Capitan in his arms.

"You must go now. Tell her, I love her. Go you must not come back to this place."

"Come with me. We can make it together."

The captain pulls out the family photo from his top pocket. He puts it in his hand.

"Go now."

He dies in his arms.

He runs for his life. He continues to hear explosives in the background. He finally arrives at the tunnel hatch. He continues to run as the tunnel begins to collapse as he reaches the other side of the border. He runs home.

"Where are you?"

"Oh, my son, you made it back. Thank God."

"I met him."

"My God. Where is he?"

Nadia's son hangs his head in sorrow.

"He saved my life. He didn't make it. His last words were to tell you he loves you."

Nadia begins to cry. She looks up as the sky begins to rumble with a sound the earth has never heard before. Nadia and her son are taken up as they disappear from where they stand.

Two men are on a roof top working. One man disappears and the other remains. A group of church members are in bible class and a few members disappear. The others remain in their sets. An airplane is flying and the pilot disappears and the passengers are aboard as the plane goes down.

People are walking in a Department Mall and some disappears and other remains. People in automobiles are driving and some in the passengers set disappears and some in the driver sets disappears. Vehicular are crashing all over the city. A family of five is in the house and one disappears and the others remain.

A poor man walks up to a rich man and asks for food and the rich man tells him to go away and find a job, and the poor man disappear. Several firemen are putting out a fire and two firemen's disappears and the other remains.

A one is operating on a patient and the patient disappears and the staff remains. A paramedic is transporting a patient as he is on life support and the driver disappears.

The world will then suffer the greatest tribulation unimaginable. Hell is unlashed and plagues and devastation will last for quite some time. In a stunning revelation as other countries begin to war against in Jerusalem, the most shocking event takes place. The earthquake, blood and fire in sky are shown and earth beneath, with vapor of smoke.

In a stunning revelation as other countries begin to war against in Jerusalem, the most shocking event takes place. The earthquake, blood and fire in sky are shown and earth beneath, with vapor of smoke. Then the sun turns into darkness, and the moon into blood. As the book of Revelations 5: 1-10 reviles the end of time, it will unfold the most shocking events man have ever known. REVELATION 5:1-10

5-1) And I saw in the right hand of him that sat on the throne a book written within and on the backside, sealed with SEVEN SEALS.

6-1) And I saw when the Lamb opened one of the seals, and I heard, as it were the noise of thunder, one of the four beasts saying, Come and see.

6-2 And I saw, and behold a white horse: and he that sat on him had a bow; and a crown was given unto him: and he went forth conquering, and to conquer.

6-3 And when he had opened the second seal, I heard the second beast say, Come and see.

6-4) And there went out another horse that was red: and power was given to him that sat thereon to take peace from the earth, and that they should kill one another: and there was given unto him a great sword.

6-5) And when he had opened the third seal, I heard the third beast say, Come and see. And I beheld, and lo a black horse; and he that sat on him had a pair of balances in his hand.

6-6) And I heard a voice in the midst of the four beasts say, A measure of wheat for a penny, and three measures of barley for a penny; and see thou hurt not the oil and the wine.

6-7) And when he had opened the fourth seal, I heard the voice of the fourth beast say, Come and see

6-8) And I looked, and behold a pale horse: and his name that sat on him was Death, and Hell followed with him. And power was given unto them over the fourth part of the earth, to kill with sword, and with hunger, and with death, and with the beasts of the earth.

6-9 And when he had opened the fifth seal, I saw under the altar the souls of them that were slain for the word of God, and for the testimony, which they held:

6-10 And they cried with a loud voice, saying, How long, O Lord, holy and true, dost thou not judge and avenge our blood on them that dwell on the earth

6-11 And white robes were given unto every one of them; and it was said unto them, that they should rest yet for a little season, until their fellow servants also and their brethren, that should be killed as they were, should be fulfilled.

6-12 And I beheld when he had opened the sixth seal, and, lo, there was a great earthquake; and the sun became black as sackcloth of hair, and the moon became as blood;

6-13 And the stars of heaven fell unto the earth, even as a fig tree casteth her untimely figs, when she is shaken of a mighty wind.

6-14 And the heaven departed as a scroll when it is rolled together; and every mountain and island were moved out of their places

6-15 And the kings of the earth, and the great men, and the rich men, and the chief captains, and the mighty men, and every bondman, and every free man, hid themselves in the dens and in the rocks of the mountains;

6-16 And said to the mountains and rocks, Fall on us, and hide us from the face of him that sitteth on the throne, and from the wrath of the Lamb:

6-17 For the great day of his wrath is come; and who shall be able to stand?

7-1 And after these things I saw four angels standing on the four corners of the earth, holding the four winds of the earth, that the wind should not blow on the earth, nor on the sea, nor on any tree.

7-2 And I saw another angel ascending from the east, having the seal of the living God: and he cried with a loud voice to the four angels, to whom it was given to hurt the earth and the sea,

7-3 Saying, Hurt not the earth, neither the sea, nor the trees, till we have sealed the servants of our God in their foreheads.

7-4 And I heard the number of them which were sealed: and there were sealed an hundred and forty and four thousand of all the tribes of the children of Israel.

7-9 After this I beheld, and, lo, a great multitude, which no man could number, of all nations, and kindreds, and people, and tongues, stood before the throne, and before the Lamb, clothed with white robes, and palms in their hands;

7-10 And cried with a loud voice, saying, Salvation to our God which sitteth upon the throne, and unto the Lamb.

7-11 And all the angels stood round about the throne, and about the elders and the four beasts, and fell before the throne on their faces, and worshipped God,

7-12 Saying, Amen: Blessing, and glory, and wisdom, and thanksgiving, and honour, and power, and might, be unto our God forever and ever. Amen.

7-13 And one of the elders answered, saying unto me, What are these which are arrayed in white robes? and whence came they?

7-14 And I said unto him, Sir, thou knowest. And he said to me, These are they which came out of great tribulation, and have washed their robes, and made them white in the blood of the Lamb.

7-15 Therefore are they before the throne of God, and serve him day and night in his temple: and he that sitteth on the throne shall dwell among them.

7-16 They shall hunger no more, neither thirst any more; neither shall the sunlight on them, nor any heat. 7-17 For the Lamb which is in the midst of the throne shall feed them, and shall lead them unto living fountains of waters: and God shall wipe away all tears from their eyes.

8-1 And when he had opened the seventh seal, there was silence in heaven about the space of half an hour. 8-2 And I saw the seven angels which stood before God; and to them were given seven trumpets.

8-3 And another angel came and stood at the altar, having a golden censer; and there was given unto him much incense, that he should offer it with the prayers of all saints upon the golden altar which was before the throne.

8-4 And the smoke of the incense, which came with the prayers of the saints, ascended up before God out of the angel's hand.

8-5 And the angel took the censer, and filled it with fire of the altar, and cast it into the earth: and there were voices, and thunderings, and lightnings, and an earthquake.

8-6 And the seven angels which had the seven trumpets prepared themselves to sound.

8-7 The first angel sounded, and there followed hail and fire mingled with blood, and they were cast upon the earth: and the third part of trees was burnt up, and all green grass was burnt up.

8-8 And the second angel sounded, and as it were a great mountain burning with fire was cast into the sea: and the third part of the sea became blood;

8-9 And the third part of the creatures which were in the sea, and had life, died; and the third part of the ships were destroyed.

8-10 And the third angel sounded, and there fell a great star from heaven, burning as it were a lamp, and it fell upon the third part of the rivers, and upon the fountains of waters;

8-11 And the name of the star is called Wormwood: and the third part of the waters became wormwood; and many men died of the waters, because they were made bitter.

8-12 And the fourth angel sounded, and the third part of the sun was smitten, and the third part of the moon, and the third part of the stars; so as the third part of them was darkened, and the day shone not for a third part of it, and the night likewise.

8-13 And I beheld, and heard an angel flying through the midst of heaven, saying with a loud voice, Woe, woe, woe, to the inhabiters of the earth by reason of the other voices of the trumpet of the three angels, which are yet to sound!

9-1 And the fifth angel sounded, and I saw a star fall from heaven unto the earth: and to him was given the key of the bottomless pit.

9-2 And he opened the bottomless pit; and there arose a smoke out of the pit, as the smoke of a great furnace; and the sun and the air were darkened by reason of the smoke of the pit.

9-3 And there came out of the smoke locusts upon the earth: and unto them was given power, as the scorpions of the earth have power.

9-4 And it was commanded them that they should not hurt the grass of the earth, neither any green thing, neither any tree; but only those men which have not the seal of God in their foreheads.

9-5 And to them it was given that they should not kill them, but that they should be tormented five months: and their torment was as the torment of a scorpion, when he striketh a man.

9-6 And in those days shall men seek death, and shall not find it; and shall desire to die, and death shall flee from them.

9-7 And the shapes of the locusts were like unto horses prepared unto battle; and on their heads were as it were crowns like gold, and their faces were as the faces of men.

9-8 And they had hair as the hair of women, and their teeth were as the teeth of lions.

9-9 And they had breastplates, as it were breastplates of iron; and the sound of their wings was as the sound of chariots of many horses running to battle.

9-10 And they had tails like unto scorpions, and there were stings in their tails: and their power was to hurt men five months.

9-11 And they had a king over them, which is the angel of the bottomless pit, whose name in the Hebrew tongue is Abaddon, but in the Greek tongue hath his name Apollyon.

9-12 One woe is past; and, behold, there come two woes more hereafter.

9-13 And the sixth angel sounded, and I heard a voice from the four horns of the golden altar which is before God,

9-14 Saying to the sixth angel which had the trumpet, Loose the four angels which are bound in the great river Euphrates.

9-15 And the four angels were loosed, which were prepared for an hour, and a day, and a month, and a year, for to slay the third part of men.

9-16 And the number of the army of the horsemen were two hundred thousand: and I heard the number of them.

9-17 And thus I saw the horses in the vision, and them that sat on them, having breastplates of fire, and of jacinth, and brimstone: and the heads of the horses were as the heads of lions; and out of their mouths issued fire and smoke and brimstone.

9-18 By these three was the third part of men killed, by the fire, and by the smoke, and by the brimstone, which issued out of their mouths.

9-19 For their power is in their mouth, and in their tails: for their tails were like unto serpents, and had heads, and with them they do hurt.

~

"Please understand. He that describes the vision in Revelation didn't fully recognize the technology of our time. Therefore, his descriptions of the army of the horsemen and them that sat on them, having breastplates of fire, and of jacinth, and brimstone: and the heads of the horses were as the heads of lions; and out of their mouths issued fire and smoke and brimstone. These descriptions of our time are known as aircrafts, missiles, bombs, lasers, and atomic type weapons."

9-20 And the rest of the men which were not killed by these plagues yet repented not of the works of their hands, that they should not worship devils, and idols of gold, and silver, and brass, and stone, and of wood: which neither can see, nor hear, nor walk:

9-21 Neither repented they of their murders, nor of their sorceries, nor of their fornication, nor of their thefts.

10-1 And I saw another mighty angel come down from heaven, clothed with a cloud: and a rainbow was upon his head, and his face was as it were the sun, and his feet as pillars of fire:

10-2 And he had in his hand a little book open: and he set his right foot upon the sea, and his left foot on the earth,

10-3 And cried with a loud voice, as when a lion roareth: and when he had cried, seven thunders uttered their voices.

10-4 And when the seven thunders had uttered their voices, I was about to write: and I heard a voice from heaven saying unto me, Seal up those things which the seven thunders uttered, and write them not.

10-5 And the angel which I saw stand upon the sea and upon the earth lifted up his hand to heaven,

10-6 And sware by him that liveth for ever and ever, who created heaven, and the things that therein are, and the earth, and the things that therein are, and the sea, and the things which are therein, that there should be time no longer:

10-7 But in the days of the voice of the seventh angel, when he shall begin to sound, the mystery of God should be finished, as he hath declared to his servants the prophets.

10-8 And the voice which I heard from heaven unto me again, and said, Go and take the little book which is open in the hand of the angel which standeth upon the sea and upon the earth.

10-9 And I went unto the angel, and said unto him, Give me the little book. And he said unto me, Take it, and eat it up; and it shall make thy belly bitter, but it shall be in thy mouth sweet as honey.

10-10 And I took the little book out of the angel's hand, and ate it up; and it was in my mouth sweet as honey: and as soon as I had eaten it, my belly was bitter.

10-11 And he said unto me, Thou must prophesy again before many peoples, and nations, and tongues, and kings.

11-1 And there was given me a reed like unto a rod; and the angel stood, saying, Rise, and measure the temple of God, and the altar, and them that worship therein.

11-2 But the court which is without the temple leave out, and measure it not; for it is given unto the Gentiles: and the holy city shall they tread under foot forty and two months.

11-3 And I will give power unto my two witnesses, and they shall prophesy a thousand two hundred and threescore days, clothed in sackcloth.

11-4 These are the two olive trees, and the two candlesticks standing before the God of the earth.

11-5 And if any man will hurt them, fire proceedeth out of their mouth, and devoureth their enemies: and if any man will hurt them, he must in this manner be killed.

11-6 These have power to shut heaven that it rain not in the days of their prophecy: and have power over waters to turn them to blood, and to smite the earth with all plagues, as often as they will.

11-7 And when they shall have finished their testimony, the beast that ascendeth out of the bottomless pit shall make war against them, and shall overcome them, and kill them.

11-8 And their dead bodies shall lie in the street of the great city, which spiritually is called Sodom and Egypt, where also our Lord was crucified.

11-9 And they of the people and kindreds and tongues and nations shall see their dead bodies three days and a half, and shall not suffer their dead bodies to be put in graves.

11-10 And they that dwell upon the earth shall rejoice over them, and make merry, and shall send gifts one to another; because these two prophets tormented them that dwelt on the earth.

11-11 And after three days and a half the Spirit of life from God entered into them, and they stood upon their feet; and great fear fell upon them which saw them.

11-12 And they heard a great voice from heaven saying unto them, Come up hither. And they ascended up to heaven in a cloud; and their enemies beheld them.

11-13 And the same hour was there a great earthquake, and the tenth part of the city fell, and in the earthquake were slain of men seven thousand: and the remnant were affrighted, and gave glory to the God of heaven.

11-14 The second woe is past; and, behold, the third woe cometh quickly.

11-15 And the seventh angel sounded; and there were great voices in heaven, saying, The kingdoms of this world are become the kingdoms of our Lord, and of his Christ; and he shall reign for ever and ever.

11-16 And the four and twenty elders, which sat before God on their seats, fell upon their faces, and worshipped God,

11-17 Saying, We give thee thanks, O Lord God Almighty, which art, and wast, and art to come; because thou hast taken to thee thy great power, and hast reigned.

11-18 And the nations were angry, and thy wrath is come, and the time of the dead, that they should be judged, and that thou shouldest give reward unto thy servants the prophets, and to the saints, and them that fear thy name, small and great; and shouldest destroy them which destroy the earth.

11-19 And the temple of God was opened in heaven, and there was seen in his temple the ark of his testament: and there were lightnings, and voices, and thunderings, and an earthquake, and great hail

Then there will be War- 6th Seal OF SIGNS IN THE STARS Rev.6:12,14

There are signs in the sun, moon and stairs.
In REV. 9:1-12 THE STARS, MOON AND SUN-SOUND OF THE 5th TRUMPT.

I then the Heaven of God will be a silents- 7th seal OF SILENTS IN HEAEN silent's.

The wrath of God takes over all mankind and there is silence in Heaven for ½ hour.

Four evil angles release to kill 1/3 of man THE 6th TRUMPT REV. 9:13-21

An army of Demonic creatures kill 1/3 of mankind. Four evil angles release to kill 1/3 of man- SOUND OF THE 7th TRUMPT Rev. 11:15-19

The end of Denials 70th week as, Sores on man-Vial #1 Rev. 16:1,2. These who has the mark of the beast will be pelages with sores as man is tortured.

The sea became blood- Vial #2 Rev. 16:3The sea became blood and all sea life dies. Rivers and fountains be became blood Vail #3

Rev. 16:4-7.

The rivers and all fountains become blood. Sun scorches man- Vail #4 Rev. 16:8,9

The sun scorches man and he wish death would take him. Darkness on the seat of Anti-Christ Vail

#5 Rev.16:10,11

There will be darkness on the seat of the Anti-Christ as he gets pains from plagues he also dies and bought back to life.

After falling over that line which defines death, the elected President is brought back to life, having been transformed into the Antichrist. Euphrates dries Vail #6 Rev. 16:12-16

The Euphrates dries and demons work miracles and deceives man to gather for the battle of Armageddon.

The false religious leader sits aside the end-time "Beast" which is the king from the north. The false prophet then gives the leaders a sign. He lifts up his hands and cause fire to come down from the sky. He persuades the nation in thinking he is a god.

He then provokes and confronts all ready–made enemies of the United Nations. And it would have the power of oil, which will be denied to its adversaries or sold to buy the weapons with which to fight them.

In Jerusalem- The destruction of the post rapture Christians by the Apostate Church lead by the Antichrist, will start completion of the Temple.

The ground-breaking of a new temple will install the Middle East peace treaty and in the Middle East worldwide the Gospel will be preached in all nations. The gospel of the kingdom is preached in the entire world for a witness unto all nations; This angers the king of the north, and the force of the king of the south is completely crushed by this power.

The king of the north then comes down "like a whirlwind" and takes over the Middle East, including the Holy Land after its election as it take control of the states and then Impose Sharia and Islamic laws discriminate against minorities, jail, and persecute- particularly Christians and Jews.

A total influence of Judah will rule Jerusalem as the End-Times of more Christians are persecuted.

Then two men who are witnesses of The Gospel of Christ are persecuted in the street.

As two Christian men preaches against the false Prophet shooting Salvation is in the name Lord of Jesus Christ are persecuted brutally in the street. They rise according to Revelation. Great armies from all nations are preparing for battle. Four great ships arise across the sun arisen from different nations in Jerusalem's off the coast of Gaza for the final desolation.

As the armies prepares for war the captain has been informed that western nations have crossed the oceans.

The ships are firing artillery on land as the Captain commands all arms prepare to strike. All missiles strike west of the border.

Jerusalem- Armageddon Rev. 19:11-21

As World War begin and the great charismatic leader (Messiah) will gather together the forces of Islam in a final (holy war) against the nations of the West, whose religion, lifestyle and Religion represent a challenge to the Islamic radicals Faith.

The Eastern gate in the walled city of Jerusalem has a very special place in biblical prophecy, for it is that gate that God will use to revile His prophetic word. It was stated, in our world history year 1967 of the Six Day War.

In the year 1967 in the occasion of the Six Day War. As the fate of the new state of Israel hung in the balance. The turning point came on June 7th when the Israeli army broke through the loins gate and returned control of the ancient city of Jerusalem to the Jewish people for the first time in 1,897 years.

A fascinating news account about one of the Jewish commando groups that had been involved in the assault that some members of the group had suggested catching the Jordanian defenders of the city off guard by blowing open the sealed Eastern Gate. But the leader of the group, an Orthodox, had vehemently protested the ideal, stating that "the Eastern gate can be opened only when the Messiah come."

The Eastern gate is the only gate of the city that leads into the Temple Mount. This gate is sealed (Ezekiel 44). The context is a supernatural tour the Lord is giving Ezekiel of the future Millennial temple 40:1-3

In chapter 43 the Lord gives Ezekiel a vision of Gods glory entering the Millennial Temple from the East Gate. The Lord than say to Ezekiel: "Son of Man this is the place of My throne and the place of the soles of my feet where I will dwell among the sons of Israel forever" (43:7)

The Lord then reveals to Ezekiel that the Eastern Gate will be closed and will not be reopened until the Messiah returns in gory. (44:1-3)

This prophecy was partially fulfilled more that 400 years ago in 1517 when the Turks conquered Jerusalem under the leadership of Suleiman the Magnificent. He commanded that the city's ancient walls be rebuilt, and in the mist of this rebuilding project, for some reason, he ordered that the Eastern Gate be sealed with stone. Legends abound as to why Suleiman closed the Gate.

The most believable one is that while the walls were being built, a rumor swept Jerusalem that the Messiah was coming. Suleiman called together some Jewish rabbis and asked them to tell him about the Messiah.

They described the Messiah as a great Military leader who would be sent by God from the east. He would enter the Eastern Gate and liberate the city from foreign control.

Suleiman then decided to put and end to Jewish hope by ordering the Eastern Gate sealed. Suleiman also put a cemetery in front of the Gate, believing that no Jewish holy man would defile himself by walking through a cemetery.

The gate has remained sealed since that time and the cemetery still block the entrance. The old walled city has eight gates, and the Eastern Gate, and it alone, is sealed- just as prophesized in Ezekiel 44. The world would call that an "amazing coincidence"

I call it "Prophecy-reveled." The Eastern Gate is proof without dough the bible is the world of God. Its sealing of the Gate is clear evidence that we are living in the end times.

The Gate wait's the return of the messiah, Then and only then, will it be open. Christ returns as the clouds roll back as it unfolds. Every eye shell sees him, and all the kindred's of the earth shell wail because of him. People are calling on the name of the Lord. People are running to the mountains and they beg for the mountains to fall on them.

CHRIST
I am Al'pha and O'me-ga, the beginning
and the ending. I am!

Christ intervenes and stops World War III. Nevertheless, these armies combine as they are gathered together to make war against Him. Christ and the chosen defeat these kings and bring back the captive of Judah and Jerusalem. Christ returns in this day as His feet stand on the Mount of Olives as the mountain splits down the middle.

It was plan in past as a grave yard is built at the foot of the outside wall and coving the entrance way was sealed to stop Jesus Christ from entering into the holy land darning His return. I say Christ has all power in his hand and not even the grave will stop his conquering power in the end and defeat all nations.

All nations are gathering as all humbly enters into millennial kingdom on earth. In the gathering of the earth Jesus Christ is seen over the world through every form of technology as Ships, and aircrafts are transporting people from all over the world to praise the Lord.

News line In today's new the world is now in the Power of the King of kings as the world Transports its way to meet the Lord and saver Jesus Christ. The gathering and Judgment of the earth's is in the hands of Lord and saver Christ.

In Jerusalem the binding of Satan emerges as an angle is sent from heaven and fight with Satan. Satan is bind for 1000 years as millennial kingdom on earth takes reign with Jesus Christ earth for 1000 years. All while life no longer feed off each other and the earth is at peace for 1000 years. Than shell come a time as never seen before and none like after for the finial release and rebellion of Satan shell abound. God has never deserted man but man has always rebelled and separated himself from God.

For whatever reason Satan is released is one of the mysteries of God. As the written scriptures states "The secrete things belong to God" And after those day had come if it wasn't for the shorting of this time the world would be no more. Judgment of Satan and the world is at hand and Satan's finial end as he is cast into the lake of fire.

Revelation 19:11

11 In revelations of John: And I saw heaven open, and behold a white horse; and he that sat upon him was called Faithful and True, and rightness he doth judge and make war.

12 His eyes were as a flame of fire, and on his head were many crowns; and he had a name written, that no man knew, but he himself.

13 And he was clothed with a vesture dipped on blood; and his name is called The Word of God.

14 And the armies which werein heaven followed him upon white horeses, clothed in find linen, white and clean.

15 And out of his month goeth a sword, that with it he should smite the nations. And he shell rule them with a rod of iron: and he treaded the winepress of the fierceness and wrath of almighty God.

16 and he has in his vesture and on his thigh a name written, KING OF KINGS AND LORD OF LORDS.

17 And I saw an angel standing in the sun, and he cried with a loud voice, saying to all the fowls that fly in the midst of heaven, Come and gather yourselves together unto the supper of the great God;

18 That ye may eat the flesh of the mighty men both free and bond, both small and great.

19 And I saw the beast, and the kings of the earth, and their armies, gathered together to make war with against him that sat on the horse, and againce his army.

20 And the beast was taken, and with him the flase prophet that wrought miracles before him, with which he deceived them that had received the mark of the beast, and them that worshipped the image. Those both were cast alive into a lake of fire burning with brimstones.

21 And the remnant were slain with the sword of him that sat upon the horse, which sword proceed out of his month: and all of the fowels were filled with their flesh.

And according to Zechariah 14:4 there will be a time when Christ shell stand in the last days.

14: 4-And his feet shall stand in that day upon the mount of Olives, which is before Jerusalem on the east, and the mount of Olives shall cleave in the midst thereof toward the east and toward the west, and there shall be a very great valley; and half of the mountain shall remove toward the north, and half of it toward the south.

Revelations: 7:9-10

9 After that I behold, and lo, a great multitude, which no man could number, of all nations, and kindred's, and people, and tongues stood before the throne, and before the lamb, clothed with white robes, and palms in their hands.

10 And cried out with a loud voice, Saying, SALVATION UNTO OUR GOD THAT SITTETH UPON THE THRONE, AND UNTO THE LAMB.

The Multitude will throw their crowns to the feet of the Lord with a shout. Glory! we are not worthy. Glory is to God! Glory is to God! Glory is to God!

God Create a new heaven and a new earth. For heaven and earth shell pass away but God's word shell last forever. And the Lord Christ shell returns all power back to the God-Head. For it is done!

For Christ will raise all the dead that lay and rest and death is no more. The destruction of the present heaven and earth shell pass away.

The great white thorn of Judgment takes places. All saints are given their rewards according to their deeds, and Saints will throw their crowns at the feet of the lord.

According to Relverlations 3:12, Christ the son of man states,:Him that overcometh will I make a pillar in the temple of my God, and he shall go no more out: and I will write upon him the name of my God, and the name of the city of my God, which is new Jerusalem, which cometh down out of heaven from my God: and I will write upon him my new name.

Dr. Yu gave me his prognosis.

"Most dreams are metaphorical and, most times, represent some underlying problems. You have come a long way from where you started. You have traveled many roads to find your way in life. You must return home and face your past, for your journey is over. You must go now, for we will never meet again. Your journey has ended."

I stood up with a puzzled look on my face and walked towards the door. I looked back and noticed that he wrote one more time on his pad.

He wrote the word "journey" in large letters.

He stood up for the first time from his seat. Then he faced me. I was even more puzzled and in a state of shock. I backed up to the door.

When I saw him, I thought, "Oh, no! It's not you. It's me."

Dr. Yu was a mirror image of me in a suit. He turned his pad towards me and said, "I am your subconscious. I'm not whom you expected to see, but you are a part of me. You are now free. Go, and meet your destiny."

He turned his pad towards me. The word he circled was "JUDGMENT." The pad now read:

T alent
N ecessity
E scape
M achine
G host
D eception
U npredictable
J ourney

I opened the door to make a quick exit. The first step out from the door, I found no floor—just a bottomless pit. I fell and continued to fall. Suddenly, I heard a pounding on the door, and it startled me awake. "Oh my God was this just a dream? I must have fallen asleep. I didn't even get a chance to say my prayers, and I missed my appointment. Well, now is a better time than any to say my prayers, but someone is still knocking on my door."

I put on my slippers and went to the front door. Everything seemed to go in slow motion. I thought, "Maybe it's my neighbor who usually comes over to drink coffee before work. I opened the door and to my surprise I saw nothing. Then I heard His words in a loud voice.

I immediately realized it was the voice of God and I was in the spiritual world.

Now I lay me down to sleep.
I pray the Lord my soul he'll keep.
For if I die before I wake,
I pray the Lord
My soul he'll take.
Amen.
Sweet Dreams.

God continues to work with man in many
ways as he did in biblical days.

3 John 1:5
Beloved, thou doest faithfully whatsoever thou doest to the
brethren, and to strangers;

3 John 1:6
Which have borne witness of thy charity before the church:
whom if thou bring forward on their journey after a godly
sort, thou shall do well.

"Make sure you're prepared for what God will keep"

Acts 2:19

And I will show wonders in heaven above, and signs in the earth beneath; blood, and fire, and vapor of smoke:

Acts 2:20

The sun shall be turned into darkness, and the moon into blood, before the great and notable day of the Lord come:

After all is said and done, I have
come to realize.
I'm just a paw
in the hands
of God.

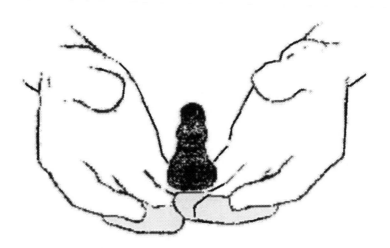

Personal Letter To the Reader:

If there are any doubts that my dreams and visions, I have kept evidence of one last dream.

Actual Event:

This is not just a story of me. This is a story of taking dreams into my hands and showing something bigger than me, for truth and righteousness are God's judgments.

One point in my life, I was expecting triplets from a love to come into our lives. On August 1, 2002, I entered a contest on the "Tom Joyner Morning Show". This was the "Tom Joyner Christmas Wish" contest. This ABC radio show gave its listeners the opportunity to write letters expressing special needs for a Christmas wish. There are thousands of daily listeners who request a Christmas wish during this contest.

After researching the contest on the internet the night before, I decided to write and submit my own Christmas wish. In reviewing the profiles of each staff member of the "Tom Joyner Morning Show", I was amazed. Each member had talents and accomplishments beyond radio broadcasting. There were photos of each radio host. One stood out more than others.

I chuckled in admiration when I saw a photo of J. Anthony Brown with a cool, old-school hat on his head. In my sleep this night, I had a dream. In this dream were three babies at birth. Upon reaching out to them, they suddenly took flight and slowly went off into the clouds. They had white wings and all of a sudden the strangest thing appeared.

They all appeared with a hat on their heads. Each one had the face of J. Anthony Brown, the same face I admired in his photo profile on the internet. I saw three dollar's fall from the sky and I awakened.

The next day I entered my letter in the Tom Joyner Christmas Wish contest. My dream was described as a part of my wish. The date was August 8, 2002 and the babies due date was during the week of my birthday. This meant that there was a possibility that they would be born on my birthday!

My letter was three-pages in length, and in my letter, I described the dream and the connection with J. Anthony Brown. Each week, I listened to the radio station and hoped for the winning opportunity. Each week a radio host selected and read a letter for a Christmas wish. What were the odds of my letter being selected in this contest for this week? To my surprise, my letter was chosen.

The selected reader for my winning letter was J. Anthony Brown. I was granted a cash prize of $2,500 and a recording of the live reading of my letter. I saw my dream after these events appear. I realize now that when I saw my babies floating away into the clouds with wings, that the dream was showing me the passing of my babies during birth. The babies remained healthy throughout the pregnancy. However, there were complications at birth and the babies did not survive. This is where I saw the babies floating away as I tried to reach for them out of the sky. When I saw the babies with the hats and face of J. Anthony Brown and three dollars fall from the sky, this represented that he would be an important part in granting my Christmas wish of winning a cash prize.

Since I was not able to use the two gift cards, which totaled $2500, I donated the two gift cards to two families, each having a set of twins.

Don't be mistaken by the fact that all of my dreams appear to be of tragedy or disappointments.

Even though, there are not many dreams of events that show happiness, my dreams normally warn me of danger. This may be because my dreams from God are for my protection and safety.

I never question God for the unfortunate events and tragedies that occur in my life. I only hope that with my dreams, I have favor of His grace. God has revealed unto me the reality of dreams by his Spirit. The Bible tells us that the Spirit searches all things, yea and the deep things of God.

Printed in the United States
By Bookmasters